I0100625

ORDERED STEPS: THE LIFE AND CAREER OF DR. AUDREY FORBES MANLEY

ORDERED STEPS: THE LIFE AND CAREER OF DR. AUDREY FORBES MANLEY

AMALIA K. AMAKI

FOREWORD BY

DR. PAMELA GUNTER-SMITH

First published in 2025
as part of the **Health, Wellness & Society Book Imprint**
doi: 10.18848/978-1-966214-47-2/CGP (Full Book)

Common Ground Research Networks
2001 South First Street, Suite 202
University of Illinois Research Park
Champaign, IL
61820

Library of Congress Cataloging-in-Publication Data

Names: Amaki, Amalia K. author
Title: Ordered steps : the life and career of Dr. Audrey Forbes Manley / by Amalia K. Amaki ; foreword by Dr. Pamela Gunter-Smith.
Description: Champaign, IL : Common Ground Research Networks, 2025. | Includes bibliographical references. | Summary: "Dr. Audrey Forbes Manley experienced a tumultuous yet remarkable journey from poverty in rural Mississippi to high-level appointments in Chicago, San Francisco, Atlanta, and Washington, D.C., where she acted as U.S. Surgeon General for over two years. Her treatment methods and research on Similac formulas saved countless babies' lives. She oversaw early fund distributions for such autosomal recessive disorders as sickle cell disease and cystic fibrosis. Her effective oversight of the Emory University/ Grady Memorial Hospital Family Planning Clinic facilitated health programs benefiting diverse communities"-- Provided by publisher.

Identifiers: LCCN 2025004876 (print) | LCCN 2025004877 (ebook) | ISBN 9781966214458 hardback | ISBN 9781966214465 paperback | ISBN 9781966214472 adobe pdf

Subjects: LCSH: Manley, Audrey F. | African American women physicians--Biography | Health officers--United States--Biography | Women pediatricians--United States--Biography | Public health administration--United States--History | LCGFT: Biographies
Classification: LCC R154.M2927 A43 2025 (print) | LCC R154.M2927 (ebook) | DDC 610.92--dc23/ eng/20250524

LC record available at https://lccn.loc.gov/2025004876
LC ebook record available at https://lccn.loc.gov/2025004877

TABLE OF CONTENTS

FOREWORD

It is both a personal and professional honor to have been asked to provide a foreword to the biography of Dr. Audrey Forbes Manley. Student, teacher, wife, sister, doctor, public servant, Spelman College Trustee, Spelman College President—she epitomizes all of these descriptors.

I first met Dr. Manley in 1970 as a biology major at Spelman College. She was newly married to Albert E. Manley, then president of the College, and had just joined him as first lady. As she tells the story, my roommates and I knocked on the door of the president's home and proceeded to tell her what we expected her to do for students in the sciences. Little did I know then that I was following in her footsteps. As a student, she, too, had told the then President Albert E. Manley what he needed to do for students in the sciences. Thus began our relationship, which now spans fifty years.

Dr. Manley's arrival at Spelman in 1970 as first lady was a pivotal moment, especially for Spelman students who aspired to move into the nontraditional fields of science and medicine. Dr. Manley was already held in high esteem. She had served as a Trustee of the College before marrying President Albert Manley. She personified a successful woman of color, one who was accomplished in her own right and who was able to balance the demands of being the spouse to the president and a physician/researcher. As such, she made improving the science curriculum one of her major causes.

It was also a time of great change within our country and the Atlanta University Center. Student activism was at an all-time high, as we discovered who we were and our own power—"Black Woman Power"—to bring about change. We joined the political arena, campaigned for Atlanta's first Black candidate for mayor, protested the Vietnam War, and, of course, embraced our role in serving our community. Audrey Manley embraced this as well.

Twenty-seven years later, in 1997, she returned to Spelman, this time as the College's eighth and first alumna president. Our paths would cross once again, as I, too, had returned to Spelman as the Porter Professor of Physiology and chair of the Biology Department, and associate provost for science and technology. As president, she renewed her commitment to the sciences by completing the capital campaign for the renovation and expansion of the science building. The facility is named the Albro-Falconer-Manley Science Center, honoring three Spelman science icons, Dr. Helen Tucker Albro, the first chair of Spelman's Biology Department; Dr. Etta Zuber Falconer, Spelman Calloway Professor of Mathematics and associate provost for science programs and policy; and Dr. Audrey Forbes Manley herself.

So how is it that Audrey Forbes Manley arrived at Spelman to lead countless young women of color to dream of possibilities? The answer is deeply rooted in her experiences forged by courage, perseverance, and resilience—what I refer to as my CPR. Behind all of her successes is a story of achievement despite the odds, and perhaps, of adversities that shaped her. Throughout her life, she created opportunities by being brave enough to launch herself into unknown, and oftentimes, uncomfortable new situations where women—especially those of color—were not welcomed.

As I read her story, I begin to understand why she is so special to me. She forged a way through uncharted territories for me and many others. I learned much from her during her tenure as a student, a staff member, and an administrator at Spelman. A night owl, Dr. Manley always took my calls, sometimes at midnight when I needed her signature on a grant I was sending to DC via courier for review. As I embarked on my own college presidency, I benefited from my observations of her as she moved her agenda for the College forward. Focused on the future, she saw her role as promoting fundraising, land acquisition, improvement of campus facilities and technology, and institutionalizing community service. I have embraced many of these as areas of emphasis for my presidency.

During my meetings in her office, Dr. Manley would normally conclude the conversation with "and you will make that happen." At the time, I considered it a directive, but I was wrong. Rather, it was a sign of the confidence that she had in me that I could accomplish what needed to be done. There was never any doubt in my mind who I would ask to speak at my inauguration as I embarked on my own college presidency: Dr. Audrey Manley, my mentor and Spelman sister, someone to whom I will always be connected. An accomplished woman with the drive to make it happen. I was so very honored to have her come and speak at my new campus home, where I am the first woman of color to be president of the institution. My hope is that my legacy will be as rich as hers, opening the doors of opportunity for other women who will make it happen!

Pamela J. Gunter-Smith, PhD
Former President
York College of Pennsylvania

INTRODUCTION

The place in which I will fit will not exist until I make it.
—James Baldwin

Given the harsh nature of Black life in Mississippi during the 1930s, it seemed unlikely that a path to high achievement in the medical field would originate in Jackson, and that a course of events would unfold where working in the cotton and corn fields of Tougaloo and serving as the US surgeon general would exist in the same African American woman's narrative. Dr. Audrey Forbes Manley went from being essentially invisible in the deep south of her youth to gaining recognition on Capitol Hill as the country's lead public health advisor. It is a story that is as much about inner strength and tenacity of the mind as it is reflective of accomplishments and advancement of a professional career. Attributing her success to divine guidance and a vow made as a preschooler that she would devote her adult life to caring for and comforting the sick, she navigated through painful family dilemmas, poverty, traumatic loss, and racial and gender bias in the pursuit of one goal—to become a doctor. By the time the likelihood that she would join physician ranks was all but a foregone conclusion, Dr. Manley had developed the additional interest in seeing more women, especially African Americans, enter the medical profession.

Thoughts turned immediately to her alma mater, Spelman College, an all-female, undergraduate HBCU (Historically Black College and Universities) in Atlanta with a good reputation for its liberal arts emphasis and impressive list of alumnae. Believing that "Spelman women should lead in this evolution in healthcare," a position she consistently expressed, Dr. Manley initiated subtle yet ongoing campaigns, advocacies, and appeals to facilitate reaching this objective.

Dr. Manley did not consider herself to be the activist or trailblazer that her track record revealed. Despite a string of African American female firsts, she remained low-keyed and faithfully followed the roads she considered were divinely laid out before her. She operated in the best interest of patients, and took on difficult tasks with commitment and diligence. Her attentiveness to childhood diseases;

research and improved treatment of infants; diminishing high mortality rates among poor, Black babies; and a host of other medical conditions threatening the lives of newborns was appropriately conjoined with issues such as teenage pregnancy, drug addiction, and life-threatening emergencies in young patients resulting from gang violence. Through it all, she envisioned a future where women, especially African American women, played more significant roles in the provision of nationwide healthcare, with Spelman graduates being prominent among them.

Dr. Manley retired only after serving Spelman for five years—improving its infrastructure, endowment, and surrounding neighborhood. Reflecting on her history of health-related world travels, military ranks, and lead federal agency positions, it became astounding even for her to recall that her point of beginning was as "a poor Black girl from Jackson, Mississippi."

CHAPTER 1

Jackson to Tougaloo

Jackson, Mississippi, in the 1930s was typically Southern—a segregated, race-conscious principality struggling to rise from underneath the economic throes of the Great Depression challenging most people to live off a near-bare minimum. It was the birthplace or adopted residence of some of America's accomplished writers who translated Jackson's social, racial, and cultural dynamics into iconic literary works. At the same time, illegal drinking and gambling flourished on the city's East side along the Pearl River. Casinos, bootleg liquor stores, and nightclubs were on a strip of black-market businesses on much of Flowood Road, which was called the Gold Coast. Although engaging in activities that were technically outside the law, the district was a thriving center of nightlife and music with many local and national blues and jazz musicians appearing regularly at a strip of clubs along Fannin Road referred to by African Americans as "cross the river."

Area rail lines including the Illinois Central provided employment opportunities for a modest number of African Americans, with a few others holding professional positions at HBCUs, but the majority worked in labor-related, farm-related, and domestic jobs. The community was the hardest hit in terms of loss of work, with half of the population being unemployed. Jim Crow disenfranchisement, restrictive boundaries, and acts of intimidation and violence against Black citizens remained common. However, in the midst of the global financial crisis, African Americans in Jackson in the mid-1930s, as elsewhere in the country, managed to eke out a reliable daily routine, and in deference to the harsh realities of the racial divide, considered the city home.

On Sunday, March 25, 1934, Audrey Elaine Forbes was born into the Black community of Jackson, Mississippi. The daughter of Iralee Buckhalter and Jesse Lee Forbes, her entry was marked by more than the segregation and poverty that would form the backdrop of her youth. There was the additional ticklish situation created by her father, a recent high school graduate who was completing his freshman year at Jackson College (now Jackson State University). Her father had gotten two other young ladies pregnant around the same time as her mother. Three concurrent pregnancies constituted a major breach of normalcy for Audrey's family, and established a foundation for awkwardness that was naturally oblivious to her during infancy, but would eventually challenge her ability to have an innocent childhood and anything near a typical adolescence.

On the other hand, Audrey was destined to grow up in the midst of elders whose deeply rooted faith was paired with the affectionate care they provided her. This grounded her in a belief in the power of self-determination. It was instilled in her that circumstances around the beginning of a person's life should not define their entire existence, destroy their dreams, or take away the ability to achieve their goals. The unusual circumstances of her early days were continually leveraged by an ability to cope due to an unwavering belief that there was a divine plan for her life.

Her mother, Iralee, grew up in a devout Catholic household where, despite having limited resources, the Buckhalter family managed to enroll Iralee in Holy Ghost Catholic School, a parochial institution founded in 1918 on what later became Cloister Street. It was the first high school constructed for African Americans in Jackson and the first accredited by the Southern Association for Secondary Schools. The other two young mothers attended Lanier High School on East Ash Street. Founded in 1925 as a junior–senior high school for seventh- through twelfth-grade students, Lanier High was the first public high school built for African Americans in Jackson.

Sue, one of the Lanier High students, lived with her family on Roosevelt Street located directly behind Audrey's father's family home. Sue gave birth to a son who, in a short period of time, apparently resembled Audrey's father so much, everyone called him Little Jesse. The second Lanier High student, Myrtle, was the youngest of four children in a middle class family that lived on another side of town. Her two brothers and only sister were well educated, highly motivated, and became established members of their chosen fields. Myrtle's brothers were graduates of Tougaloo College and Meharry Medical College—one in medicine and the other in dentistry. Her sister finished Tougaloo and became an educator and civil rights activist who led the statewide campaign for Black teachers in Mississippi to receive equal pay as their White counterparts. Myrtle, being still in high school, drew the wrath of her father when he learned about her pregnancy.

Myrtle's father was a hardworking postal employee who made the mail run from Jackson to Chicago on the Panama Limited railroad. His strong work ethic and strict Christian upbringing fueled his contention that Myrtle's actions were inappropriate, inexcusable, and intolerable. As head of the family, he ordered Myrtle out of the house, forbidding her to ever return. With no other place to go, she moved into the Forbes home, subsequently giving birth to a daughter named Gwendolyn (Gwen) Yvonne. Three weeks later, Myrtle was discovered dead, holding Gwen in her arms.

Myrtle's move into the Forbes house was unsettling for Iralee's family, especially Audrey's grandmother. Consequently, Minnie Davis Buckhalter made the corporate decision to raise Audrey as her own daughter. In the discreet arrangement, Audrey initially grew up believing Iralee, her eighteen-year-old biological mother, was her older sister. She was further led to believe her eleven-year-old uncle, John, who was born to a youthful Minnie at age forty-two, was her brother. Unable to break the habit, she called her uncle "Brother" for the rest of his life. Her maternal great-grandmother, Dora Davis, completed the close circle of people in the home who, for her, were immediate family. It was a smooth, workable, and seemingly seamless plan, until the unexpected happened. Iralee became pregnant a second time, resulting in her joining Jesse at the Forbes home. She gave birth to another daughter, Barbara Juliette. It was the first in a series of events that altered the nature of the closely knit family life that two-year-old Audrey had become accustomed to and depended on.

The greater trauma occurred in1938 when her grandmother, Minnie, became critically ill. The family's presumption that she was diabetic and had slipped into a coma one night was incorrect. They soon learned she suffered from hypertension, and the condition had led to a stroke. On the fateful evening, as Minnie lay in pain in a resumed state of consciousness, she insisted that some-one "bring her the baby," meaning Audrey. Audrey was scooped up and carried to her grandmother's bedside. Audrey remained quiet as she was held high and her grandmother prayed; then, being empathetic far beyond her years, she made Minnie a promise: "When I get to be big, I'm going to be a doctor so I can take care of people like you when they get sick."[1] As innocent as it seemed, the state-ment confirmed the degree of closeness between Audrey and her grandmother, and established the foundation of her intent to one day make a difference in the lives of sick people. Her life's goal was set at age four.

When an ambulance arrived, Audrey was alarmed by the state of emergency that made immediate medical assistance necessary and simultaneously intrigued by the dramatic scene that unfolded around her. Two White male paramedics rushed into the house wearing bright white jackets and slacks. They quickly attended to her grandmother before they lifted her onto a stretcher, rolled her outside, and placed her into the ambulance. They slammed the doors shut with deliberation, jumped inside, and sped off in a flurry of siren noise and strobing red lights. No one spoke. She was frozen by uncertainty as the sight and sound of those moments were, to her, totally surreal. It was the last time she saw her grandmother. It was the day that shattered her youthful sense of home.

With Minnie's loss, Audrey was sent to live with Jesse and Iralee at the Forbes home. The decision was surprising and confusing to her, being heartbroken due to her grandmother's absence, and incapable of fully comprehending the basis for her separation from the "Momma" she so deeply loved. In the new living situation, Audrey was introduced to her paternal grandmother, who everyone called "Big Momma," and her grandfather, Buck Forbes, who was called Poppa. There was the additional discovery of two siblings she never knew had existed—Barbara Juliette who was two years younger than her, and Myrtle's daughter, Gwendolyn Yvonne (Gwen), who was her same age. She would learn years later that Myrtle's mysterious death was likely suicide.

The finite nature of death was an elusive concept for Audrey during the transition, especially as it related to her grandmother, whose absence led her to inquire incessantly, "When is Momma coming to get me?" Aware that Minnie meant the world to her daughter, responding with brutal honesty was not an option Iralee ascribed to. Jesse, however, approached the situation differently, bluntly iterating that Minnie was gone forever and fiercely demanding that Audrey accept the reality that they were her parents. In fact, he insisted on her full compliance with the new family structure. When Audrey resisted, he tried to physically beat the habit out of her, instructing her with each blow that she must call Iralee "mother" and him "daddy," not Jesse. The first episode left welts and bruises over much of her body, but she held on to her own ideas about them. In fact, his brutality seemed to harden her resistance even more into adamantly declaring, "I don't care what you say. I don't care how much you beat me. Iralee will never be my mother and you will never be my father."

Retreating to a bedroom toward the rear of the house where her newly discovered sisters lingered, she entered the room as Gwen and Barbara sat motionless and stunned by what they heard and the evidence of abuse on her body. They asked nothing, but their horrified expressions begged to know *what happened?* Audrey responded in kind, not speaking one word, suffering in silence.

Over time she adapted to the new ordinary forced upon her. The next three years were less eventful, almost to the point of being mundanely routine. Audrey was compliant but not happy. She painfully grew to accept the loss of Minnie, which made the redirection of her thoughts about Iralee and Jesse somewhat more plausible, though not easier. Audrey became very fond of Little Jesse, who made regular visits to play patty-cake, hopscotch, marbles, and other children's games with her, Gwen, and Barbara in the yard and under the house. When she was seven, after Thanksgiving had recently passed and Christmas was approaching, her life suddenly changed again. It, too, was unimaginable.

On Sunday morning, December 7, 1941, just before 8 am, Japanese fighter planes bombed Pearl Harbor, a US naval base near Honolulu, Hawai'i. The next day, everyone heard reports of President Franklin Delano Roosevelt's request for Congress to declare war on Japan. In a radio address two days after the attack, the president prepared the nation for war, "urging the country to steel itself for casualties and setbacks and prepare to make the sacrifices necessary in the coming fight," adding that "Italy and Germany were continued grave threats to the United States."[2] Innocence did not buffer her from the impact of his words and the anxiety that rose among everyone around her. When, on December 11, President Roosevelt asked Congress for a declaration of war against Germany and Italy, Audrey sensed the deepening tension consuming her surroundings, and somehow knew her life was about to change.

The nation's entry into World War II spawned another exodus of African Americans from the south and rural regions to northern and eastern cities. Jobs became abundant in such locations where weapons and military supplies were being manufactured. Jesse and Iralee decided quickly to join their ranks. Like so many other young couples, they needed more lucrative work and hoped to find a better social climate in which to live. The chosen destination for African Americans migrating from Mississippi was Chicago, and Iralee and Jesse decided to go ahead alone, and relocate the rest of the family once they secured better paying jobs and a suitable place to live.

Prior to leaving for Chicago, Jesse moved his parents, Audrey, Gwen, and Barbara to Tougaloo, the nearby rural community around Tougaloo College. Their relocation was supported by President Roosevelt's "Forty-Acres and a Mule Plan," which provided recipients with forty acres of land, cattle, horses, hogs, chickens, and educational assistance from home economics professionals. In her family's case, the assigned home economics representative taught her grandmother food canning techniques so that their fall harvests could feed them sufficiently throughout winter. It took a few months for the family to reasonably settle in, after which Jesse and Iralee left for Chicago.

Despite being in close proximity to one another, Jackson and Tougaloo seemed worlds apart to Audrey. The house they left in Jackson, though modest, had utilities, bathroom facilities, running water, and was a part of a legitimate neighborhood. However, rent had to be paid. In Tougaloo, they moved into a free-use, large rural house at the railroad station that was built originally for people who worked for the industry. There was no electricity, running water, or indoor toilets. Instead, there was an outhouse, and a well that was dug for water, and wood was cut for heat and cooking. With the nation at war, everyone in the area worked hard to survive. News updates about the war came from President Roosevelt's fireside radio chats broadcast on Friday nights. No one living in rural Tougaloo had a radio at home, being without electricity. To hear the president's messages, her family, along with all of their neighbors, walked to the community grocery store, congregated outside, and sat on wooden crates or whatever else was available to listen to the broadcasts.

They lived in the shadows of Tougaloo College. To Audrey, the school was a beacon on a hill. A private, coeducational, four-year church related liberal arts institution, Tougaloo College sat on 500 acres of land on West County Line Road—the marker between the two cities—in the unincorporated area historically designated as the Tougaloo area of Jackson, Mississippi. Founded in 1869, the college was located ten miles north of downtown Jackson, just across the county line in Madison County. As was typical with HBCUs at the time, maintaining grammar and high schools provided a place for their students to practice-teach while simultaneously meeting educational needs of the Black community. HBCUs were primarily graduating teachers at the time, and their students were not allowed to practice-teach in public schools in the region; plus, those systems did not pay anything.

Audrey had the advantage of entering third grade on the campus at Daniel Hand Grammar School where there were very good teachers. There was one problem. The school did not focus on young people from the local rural community. Instead, Daniel Hand was intended for children of the few Black professionals in Tougaloo and Jackson, i.e., doctors, lawyers, and academicians such as deans and faculty at Jackson State, Alcorn State, and Tougaloo Colleges (now Universities) who paid tuition. Their sons and daughters filled the majority of the classrooms with only a handful of students coming from the nearby community. Audrey and her sisters were among the few allowed to enter, although the expected student body was always made clear. Preference was given to the other students in all aspects of classroom interaction, a constant reminder of who the school was there for.

As a rule, teachers ignored Audrey during class discussions, even when her hand was raised.

Another advantage to being near the college was experiencing campus events, albeit vicariously. There were always activities at Tougaloo, the school being a center of cultural life. A common pastime for curious young people was hanging over the college fence to watch whatever was occurring, whether observing people moving to and from concerts, sports activities like basketball and football games, or any number of happenings. A high point of her first year there was catching views of an academic processional. The image of students in caps and gowns marching against the backdrop of meticulously manicured grounds before entering Woodworth Chapel to the sound of organ music made quite the impression. While the ceremony was common practice at colleges and universities, it was Audrey's first chance to witness it firsthand. Somehow in the midst of those moments, she knew that one day she, too, would participate in such a ritual.

Tougaloo's campus was the congregating spot for young locals on Sunday afternoons. They would ride bicycles and skate on the property, since it was the only place around with sidewalks. Woodworth Chapel was the venue for most of the college's cultural, social, and political activity. Concerts and lectures at Woodworth included appearances by such renowned figures as lyric tenor and composer Roland Hayes, contralto Marian Anderson, and Star Bronze Medal recipient and future US Senator Edward William Brooke III. Gaining exposure, though indirectly, to the impressive visitors who came to the institution made it even more appealing to young people like Audrey. Being a focal place in the community brought the institution to the attention of undesirable forces as well.

Tougaloo College was the target of acts of racial hatred. The Ku Klux Klan rose up whenever a prominent African American speaker was scheduled. Public announcements of their upcoming appearances at the college typically prompted the group to stage a conspicuous march through the rural community and up to the campus to characteristically burn a cross in front of the main gate. As they passed along County Line Road, Big Momma screamed desperately for Audrey and her sisters to "get under the bed!" It always amazed Audrey how efforts to intimidate the college were of little effect. After the Klan left campus, Tougaloo staff gathered at the main gate, cleaned up the entrance, and the event was held as planned.

The pace of classes during Audrey's fifth- and sixth-grade years caused her to exhibit atypical behavior at school. Teachers developed curricula in line with the abilities of the majority of the students and according to established grade level standards. Compliance with applicable lesson plans was problematic for Audrey, who was a fast learner, already advanced in her studies, eager to learn more than required, and looked forward to being increasingly challenged with each grade advancement. Completing assignments well before her classmates and wanting everyone to know it, she was prone to express her boredom and irritation with excessive talking and openly reading *All True Romance* or other comic books that were kept on hand by classmates. She was repeatedly sent to the principal's office, then home, without being allowed to return until Big Momma showed up at the school to get her back in. As embarrassing as being sent home was, the approach did not alter her behavior.

Officials at Daniel Hand were unaware of the extent to which Audrey relied on the positive affirmation and distraction that meeting tough challenges at school provided. Family instability and uncertainty about when, or if, she would join her mother in Chicago was a grave concern. She missed Iralee, and like Gwen and Barbara, was eager to leave Mississippi to start a new life in Chicago. Their constant nagging was, "When are we going to Chicago? Well, they're going to send for us this year." However, another year passed and they did not go. They believed the following year would be it. Again, they did not go. The pattern of hope turning into anticipation followed by disappointment persisted from Audrey's third through ninth grade years, the most anxious being during fifth and sixth grades.

For a time, she believed the explanation was financial. That idea was dispelled once she learned the delay had to do with their grandmother. Since Myrtle's death, Big Momma considered Gwen her child, and did not want to be apart from her. Jesse decided the three girls should not be separated, and therefore, if all of them could not go, all would have to stay. This irritated Audrey, since Jesse, to her mind, did not consider how the decision was adversely affecting Iralee, who wanted her children with her. His refusal to at least send for her and Barbara led to constant battles, fueled more by Big Momma's unwavering declaration whenever the subject came up that "Gwen cannot go." Their differences of opinion on the reunion was exacerbated by Jesse's incessant philandering.

Things were not easy for Audrey over subsequent years even though her attitude changed and her behavior improved. She remained attentive to school studies, read lots of books and indulged in a few select activities at school. She later learned from her brother (uncle) that teachers at Tougaloo noticed how advanced she was by the start of her second year, and arranged for her to skip the fifth grade, but were prevented from doing so by her father. Jesse vetoed the plan from Chicago, insisting, again, that Audrey and Gwen stay together—a move he made, according to Audrey, "without knowing everything." Jesse did not invest time in learning about the quality of their school life. He had no knowledge of the fact that from the moment she and Gwen entered third grade, being the same age and in the same class created an uncomfortable situation for them. They were constantly questioned by classmates about how, as sisters, they were in the same grade. Audrey knew they asked solely to be hurtful, but, nonetheless, repeatedly explained: "We have the same father. We don't have the same mother." Some students went so far as to spread rumors that Audrey, who was slightly taller than Gwen, must have either missed or failed a grade. As annoying as the experience was for her personally, she believed it had the greater negative impact on Gwen. The awkwardness persisted until the end of high school.

To her surprise, there were also uncomfortable moments because of her strong academic performance. Her excellence with classwork was far from secret, but it gave her no social advantage. She was usually ignored by fellow classmates and was often subjected to benign neglect on the part of her teachers. Once, during her eighth grade year when standardized national exams were given, the same test was administered to eighth-, ninth-, and tenth-grade students. Her exceptional test scores were noted quickly by administrators and staff to the delight of her homeroom teacher, Ms. Jones. Shortly after, Ms. Jones announced to the class: "I think you will be happy to know that one of *your* classmates made the highest score on the national test of all three grades in the school. Guess who it was?" Audrey sat motionless and silent as every member of the class from well-to-do families called out each other's names one by one until they were all mentioned. When Ms. Jones finally informed them, "No, it was Audrey," there was total silence, blank faces, no expression of happiness for her and no celebration. It seemed as if things went back to usual in a second.

It was her science teacher that year who proved to be a major source of inspiration and encouragement. Professor Charles Caldwell was recognized as a brilliant, multi-talented instructor with a natural ability for motivating students to reach their potential. He taught math and science classes to eighth through twelfth grades, including algebra, biology, geometry, chemistry, and physics. He took a special interest in Audrey right away. Mr. Caldwell made her time at school tolerable. He advised her to avoid being shy about doing well at school, challenged her to move above and beyond assigned tasks on her own according to her abilities, and convinced her that the only limitations before her were those she imposed on herself.

One Sunday afternoon he spotted Audrey riding a bicycle and playing with other young people in usual weekend fashion on Tougaloo's campus. Mr. Caldwell all but chastised her for being there stating, "It's all right for them to be out here riding a bicycle, but it's not all right for you. You've got bigger and better things to do. You need to be somewhere reading a book." In class, when he gave an assignment and Audrey, as usual, was the first to finish, he looked up, noticed she was done, and asked, "Audrey, have you finished?" When she answered, "Yes, sir" he said, "Well, go to the board and put it on the blackboard." At other times he said, "Go to the next chapter. Read the next chapter and be ready to tell the class what the next chapter is about." He never allowed her to waste time, making it clear there was always more work to do. His mantra was: "You finished that? Well, there's more to do, so get to work on the next one." Rather than being bothered or intimidated, she thought it was great. She loved the way Mr. Caldwell pushed her, and she rose to the challenge every time.

In retrospect, she realized her fifth- and sixth-grade teachers had no way of knowing the underlying personal reasons for her misconduct, or that they were oblivious to the fact that they ignored her in class because she lived in the rural area, or that they were unaware of the isolation and pressures she endured from other students who envied her ability to excel in class. She reflected on the fact that Tougaloo had a bus. Mr. Smith, the driver, brought students from Jackson to school every morning. At three o'clock each afternoon, he drove them back to nice homes with living rooms, dining rooms, kitchens, bathrooms, running water, and many more. When Audrey left school, she went to the fields and worked alongside her grandfather until the end of the day. If that meant picking cotton or chopping corn, that was what she did. As industrious as farm labor was from the standpoint of making her family self-sufficient, it was a dramatic contrast from the norm of classmates. On the other hand, it instilled a work ethic in her that would be valuable throughout her career.

Her grandfather was proficient at planting, tending and harvesting nearly everything they ate and needed. He understood why the land in Mississippi was not conducive to growing wheat, making it necessary for them to purchase the flour needed to make biscuits, which were a staple. Having an abundance of sugar and molasses was also important, and he knew how to grow sugarcane, take it to the mill, and boil it down to the bottom to make brown sugar. They had an abundant garden of vegetables, an orchard of fruit trees, and a hefty watermelon patch. They had nearly everything needed in terms of food and clothing which were made. Her grandmother mastered the art of caning and storing food in mason jars for winter. A hog was slaughtered in October to make ham, pork, and other things stored in the smokehouse. There was a chicken coop, from which fresh eggs were collected every morning for breakfast and as needed for baking; and chickens were selected for frying every Sunday for dinner. A cow provided sufficient milk for daily consumption, churning for butter, and making ice cream for Sunday desserts. Being wartime, most merchandise was in limited supply in stores and was, therefore, rationed, including shoes, sugar, and bacon. However, Audrey's family survived the shortages very well because her grandfather knew the measures to take to meet their needs.

A favorite time for the family was evenings when they gathered around their large fireplace roasting peanuts or sweet potatoes on hot coals while her grandfather told stories. He was a great storyteller whose attention to small details and extensive travel history gave depth and breadth to his colorful delivery. Audrey and her sisters usually coaxed him with such lead-ins as, "Poppa, tell us about when you were in St. Louis." He would quickly comply, giving them specific information about the four days of racial violence that left 200 African Americans dead and prompted 6,000 others—half of the Black population—to flee East St. Louis, Illinois in 1917.[3] He was there when the riots started and witnessed much of the dramatic developments firsthand.

When her grandfather initially told them about Lake Pontchartrain (which is actually an estuary in southeastern Louisiana), Audrey thought it was such an odd name that it could not possibly be a real location. She told him, "Poppa, you're making that up; there's no such place." He assured her, "No, there is a Lake Pontchartrain and a lot of Indians once lived around there." To her surprise, it turned out to be true. Native Americans were the original inhabitants of the area. It was called Okwa-ta, meaning wide water, by inhabitants including the Bayougoula, Mougoulacha, Chitimacha, Oumas, Tangipahoa, Acolapissa, and Quinipissalive people.

Christmastime was always special. Although the holiday in some ways accentuated the degree of their financial limitations, it was a season when warm memories were formed that endured in her mind for long periods of time. Her grandfather faithfully brought home a beautiful, freshly cut tree that was decorated with handmade ornaments since they had no funds for store-bought decorations. Being without electricity, there was not the usual dramatic effect from tree lights, especially at night; but she and her sisters were grateful for what they had and remained in high spirits because her grandparents did such a good job of taking care of them.

Iralee and Jesse had secured jobs with a manufacturer of military uniforms in Chicago, and managed to visit them almost once a year. When Audrey was twelve, her father made the trip alone. He took Audrey aside to discuss her mother's absence, informing her that Iralee was not doing well health-wise. According to him, Iralee's nerves were so bad the doctor had to put her in a nursing home where she could get the proper needed rest. Based on Jesse's report, Audrey envisioned a nice, quiet, serene, and picturesque environment with lots of green grass and trees. Later, she discovered her mother's condition was much more serious than Jesse had indicated. This reality triggered recollections of childhood experiences she had tried desperately to suppress, memories of the physical violence she, and even more so, Iralee endured from Jesse.

News stories and special reports aired on television about domestic violence always rang close to home for her because of the horrible family situation perpetuated by a father she hardly knew. She never discovered what made him the abusive, angry man he had become, since he never talked about himself, his childhood, what it was like for him growing up, or where he actually came from. Even after eventually learning he had been adopted, she still could not get to the bottom of his behavior after living with his parents who were patient, caring, and provided a good home for her and her sisters. Jesse was nothing like them. He had a terrible temper and was prone to act on it.

Audrey concluded her mother's condition was brought on by being in Chicago without the care and support of her family; that living in an environment where there was continuous disagreement, infidelity on her father's part and beatings drove her to a point of ill mental health. Audrey often noted that, while there had been considerable work done over the years addressing ways to help parents deal with special needs children, no comparable attention had been given to developing means to support or assist children, like herself, who had special needs parents. She understood that Jesse, being such a violent person, was ill-prepared for fatherhood, and her mother, as a victim of his abuse, had emotionally succumbed to the trauma of his beatings. Audrey acknowledged how she, too, had remained silent about having experienced her own share of beatings out of feelings of total helplessness, being unaware of any place of refuge for Black children caught in a family situation like hers. She was convinced her survival was because of divine covering; that, in her words, "The Lord just had His hands on me. There was no other explanation."

News of her mother's illness motivated her even more to pursue the healthcare field, even though she had fleeting moments when she wondered just how difficult it would be to achieve. At one point, she discussed possibilities with a classmate, Patricia Bell, who insisted Black women could become healthcare professionals. Patricia was a commuting student whose parents arranged for her to live with a local family while attending the Tougaloo College school during the week, and returned home every weekend. Audrey watched the close interaction between Patricia and her father when he picked her up on Fridays; heard about him taking her with him to wrestling matches on the way home to Canton, Mississippi, nineteen miles away; and noticed their warm goodbyes after he drove her back to Tougaloo every Sunday evening in time for school on Monday. It was a stark contrast to her relationship with Jesse but offered a glimpse of alternative possibilities in family relationships. Patricia enlightened her about women in health-related fields as well, pointing out to her that her aunt, like her father, was a dentist. She went on to show Audrey photographs of her aunt in a white jacket while a student at Meharry Medical College.

The image was impressive and convincing. Audrey had only been aware of men in medical roles while living in Jackson and Tougaloo up to that time. In her previous paradigm, professional women were educators, the expectation people had for her. She remained faithful to a commitment to medicine and the promise she made to Minnie. After conversing with Patricia, she began to feel unstoppable. It was 1947.

CHAPTER 2

Bound for My Promised Land

During the summer, Big Momma became so ill that Jesse had no choice but to send for them. Leaving her grandfather behind, Audrey, her grandmother, Gwen, and Barbara boarded the train in Jackson bound for the Promised Land the sisters had talked and dreamed about for seven years. Many uncles and cousins had already moved to the city, but this was their turn, finally. She would later equate the episode with certain situations in Nicholas Lemann's *New York Times* bestseller, *The Promised Land: The Great Black Migration and How It Changed America*. To her, aspects of the text resonated deeply with the account of her own journey.[1] The emotional rollercoaster of anticipation and shattered hope they had endured over the years made the final reality of the journey that much sweeter.

They carried shoebox lunches with them packed with deviled eggs, fried chicken, and ham sandwiches, sufficient food for the long ride, since African Americans were not allowed to go to the service car. Denial of access to food services on the train was a situation that was minimized by their excitement of traveling to their future home in Chicago. Further, they looked forward to chances to dine in public restaurants without racial incidence. Most of all, Audrey envisioned a large house with many rooms, indoor plumbing, and all the extras they did not have in the rural space they left behind.

Jesse picked them up at the train station and took them to his apartment—a kitchenette on the South Side where he lived with his girlfriend. Audrey was disappointed at the sight of both the space and the presence of a woman other than her mother. They were told to call his girlfriend Miss Helen. The presence of Helen in deference to that of Iralee posed a major issue for Audrey. She was disturbed by thoughts of her mother being sick and alone in a nursing home without family oversight, and the need to know exactly what her mother's condition was and the nature of her treatment and care. Audrey's persistent questions about Iralee's placement at Manteno State Hospital, and the distrust of her father's girlfriend in general strained the relationship between her, Jesse, and Helen over the next three years.

Despite the unpleasant climate in her home, Audrey remained confident that Chicago would fulfill certain childhood expectations. The area where they lived was called by the media as the "Black Belt," referring to the influx of southern and rural Blacks to the community during the war. The reference was objected to by outspoken residents until eventually, the cluster of neighborhoods became known as Bronzeville. Attracting a diversity of creative people, the community developed into a social, cultural, and economic center of Black urban life in Illinois.

Bronzeville was home to the influential *Chicago Defender*, the nationally regarded newspaper founded in 1905, and historic churches, including Olivet Baptist, Pilgrim Baptist, and Quinn Chapel African Methodist Episcopal (AME), which collectively drew thousands of worshippers to their sanctuaries each Sunday. The South Side Community Art Center on South Michigan Avenue would become a major hub for artists' engagement and the site where a number of celebrated visual artists launched their careers, including Charles White, Archibald Motley, and Gordon Parks.[2] The Savoy Ballroom, located on South Parkway (now Martin Luther King, Jr. Drive) and 47th Street, was one of the city's top night spots that showcased the nation's hottest jazz bands and performers. The nearby Regal Theater was considered the apex of entertainment in Chicago, and hosted some of the most famous Black entertainers in America, Cab Calloway, Louis Armstrong, Lena Horne, Dinah Washington, and Duke Ellington among them.

Audrey saw her first live show at the Regal Theater when singer Lou Rawls returned to do a hometown concert. She was as fascinated with his stage attire, as she was his velvety baritone voice. "He came out in a sequined jacket with bling everywhere that reacted to the stage lights with his every move. It was the most spectacular site I had ever witnessed."

Weekends were designated for sightseeing and discovering the range of cultural gems Chicago offered. Going on explorations as a family made her feel like a part of something major league. Her father essentially served as their tour guide, making a point of taking her, Gwen, and Barbara to places such as the Museum of Science and Industry, Field Museum, Planetarium, and Buckingham Fountain downtown. Venturing downtown was memorable, since the only time Audrey went downtown in Jackson was to buy a Girl Scout uniform.

Living on the seventh floor of a nine-story building, their small unit had window views of neighborhood streets stretching several blocks. The community of housing structures primarily like the one her family occupied was a stark contrast to the picturesque "Promised Land" she envisioned prior to her arrival. Despite being young, she understood the implications of being Black and living in Chicago. The economic and racial dynamics were indisputable. Audrey noticed especially how people on the South Side did not venture south of 51st Street or east of Cottage Grove Avenue without fear of negative consequences. It was one of the up-South realities of daily life for Blacks in the city that could not be ignored in the midst of the positive aspects of her new life.

In terms of education, there were three four-year public high schools in Chicago for African Americans, all located in South Side neighborhoods. Wendell Phillips High School (currently Wendell Phillips Academy High School) was named for Boston-based abolitionist, crusader, and orator Wendell Phillips (1811–1884), who openly criticized President Abraham Lincoln for delaying the emancipation of slaves. Referred to simply as Phillips, the school was founded in 1904 on 39th Street off what is currently Martin Luther King, Jr. Drive. Phillips was the first high school constructed in the area and the first predominantly African American high school in the city.[3] Jean Baptiste Point DuSable High School (aka DuSable High) was initially called the New Wendell Phillips when it opened in 1935 at 4934 South Wabash Avenue. The school was renamed in 1936 to honor the first permanent non-indigenous settler in Chicago and founder of the city, Jean Baptiste Point DuSable (1745–1818). The increasing student population at Phillips made construction of DuSable High necessary.[4] Paul Lawrence Dunbar Vocational High School, named for the influential 19th century African American poet, novelist, and playwright, was the technical school in the system. Established in 1942, Dunbar High was generally considered the vocational branch of Wendell Phillips.

In the fall, Audrey's youngest sister Barbara was enrolled in Melville W. Fuller Elementary School, which was constructed in 1884 at 4214 South Saint Lawrence Avenue at East 42nd Street. Established as Oakland School No. 2, the name was changed in 1891 in honor of Melville Weston Fuller (1833–1910), who served as the eighth Chief Justice of the United States (1888–1910). The school was completely replaced in 1942.

Audrey and Gwen were registered at Phillips, despite strong urgings from one of Jesse's friends to use someone else's address in order to enroll them in Hyde Park High School in Woodlawn. Another Southside neighborhood institution, Hyde Park was still a majority White, mixed-race high school despite the onset of a demographic transition. Jesse's friend's contention that it was a better school carried no weight with her father, who bluntly responded, "Oh, no, Wendell Phillips is fine." To her, the reply reflected her father's cavalier attitude about everything, especially education. So, discussion closed. They went to Wendell Phillips.

The walk to school was not short, but it was manageable. They began attending school two weeks after Phillips started. Audrey was particularly aware of the need to adjust to the sheer larger numbers of students in attendance after coming from smaller classes in Mississippi. Despite being confident of her level of preparedness for coursework at the new school, she still wondered about the degree to which she would measure up academically—who and how many others were among the strongest students. Concerns were dismissed after the first marking period. She made all A's, and discovered there were a handful of other outstanding classmates at the school. One was Alfreda Duster, the granddaughter of investigative journalist, educator, and activist Ida B. Wells (1862–1931). Alfreda's parents were Chicago civic leader Alfreda Barnett Duster (1904–1983) and Benjamin Cecil Duster, Jr., a World War I veteran, law clerk, and publisher. Audrey and Alfreda became fast friends, both giving highest priority for academic achievement.

Some of the other students participated in activities with groups, like Reserve Officers' Training Corps (ROTC), or bands. A contingent of students had jobs they rushed off to after school, in contrast to those who hung out together to casually socialize, experiment with marijuana, or engage in various additional activities that she and Alfreda bypassed. Phillips offered some appealing extracurricular options that the previous school did not. However, she felt Tougaloo had strong academics, which she considered to be a "straight A, B, C, geometry, trigonometry, chemistry curriculum."[5]

Although she joined the Girls Club, sang in the a cappella girls' choir, and worked on the school newspaper (where she became editor of the front page), Audrey appreciated equally the advantages afforded her at Tougaloo. She realized that Tougaloo made up for having fewer extracurricular activities with educational strengths. Within a relatively short period of time, Audrey recognized how much easier the coursework was at Phillips. Remaining at the top of her classes had been an ongoing challenge at Tougaloo. They were challenges she met, but the material became increasingly more demanding each year. Some of her classmates at Phillips struggled with work that came easy to her. There were occasions when she had already covered material at Tougaloo that students at Phillips were just being introduced to. At Phillips, she was impressed most with the mathematics instruction, acknowledging the demanding nature of the advanced courses in geometry, trigonometry, and college prep algebra. The majority of students avoided many of the math classes. Audrey took them all.

One memorable teacher from high school was Miss Harris, a young woman who had recently graduated from Talladega College in Alabama. She gave Audrey the only "B" ever received on an assignment. The delayed time it took her transcripts to arrive from Tougaloo—a mandatory prerequisite for enrollment—caused Audrey to begin taking classes two weeks late at Phillips. Miss Harris had already assigned students to work on the Leaf Project, a routine assignment at most high schools at the time. The assignment required students to collect leaves from trees, press them in books, mount the flattened objects on paper, and label them according to their botanical classification. It was a biology project that typically took two weeks. Her classmates were near completion of the project when Audrey enrolled. She persevered and managed to meet the deadline in the two days that remained. To her disappointment, Miss Harris reasoned that while Audrey had completed the assignment by the due date, theoretically having earned an "A," in the interest of fairness, it was necessary to give her a "B" because she came in late. Audrey had no choice but to accept her teacher's decision, and went on to earn an "A" for the course.

Before long, she received the hurtful news of Big Momma's declining health. Her grandmother was admitted to Cook County Hospital and diagnosed with colorectal cancer. The necessary surgery was performed, followed by chemotherapy. Once the prognosis was understood, and the nature of her post-operative needs ironed out, it was decided that Audrey would play a role in her grandmother's care when she was released to return home.

As the oldest (by a few weeks) and the one who always kept on top of her school work, Audrey was considered the best equipped of the daughters to periodically miss days of school without falling behind. Responsibility for getting Big Momma to scheduled doctor's visits became one of her primary tasks. The ritual required her to rise early enough to get herself ready, wake up her grandmother to be bathed, dressed, and fed before their walk to public transportation. They changed from the L train to the bus, and made the final walk from the bus drop-off to County Hospital.

After checking Big Momma in, and watching a nurse take her to the back, Audrey typically sat in the waiting area in a state of numbness. The reality of her grandmother's condition, the mental weight of being her commuter caretaker, and the waiting room environment were a lot to bear. She empathized with each patient who cried out in pain, overheard through the closed examination room doors. She watched sympathetically as doctors hurried back and forth along the hallway between rooms. Audrey's passion for wanting to attend to sick people intensified with every episode, causing her intent to join physician ranks to deepen. Further, the routine hospital visits stirred up thoughts of her mother Iralee.

She continued to put pressure on Jesse, asking, "When are you going to take me to see mother?" Iralee held the title fully by this time, and Audrey had a desperate need to reconnect with the mother she had not seen for years. She wanted to investigate Iralee's medical status for herself. The request was more like a demand, and she never imagined doing so would place her on a traumatic track emotionally comparable to that experienced with her grandmother when she was four. However, she had to see her mother. She was driven.

Eventually, Jesse adhered. He borrowed a friend's car and drove Audrey to Manteno, the state mental hospital in a rural Illinois Village in Kankakee County where her mother had been placed. Without expressways, it was an hour-long surface drive each way. Arriving on the grounds of the facility, her initial reaction was that the campus seemed very peaceful, pretty, and conducive to healing. After registering at the administration building and being directed to a dormitory called Barton Hall, her perception changed. She gave the following account of the experience:

> Entering Barton Hall was like walking into the scene from the movie *Snake Pit* (1948) where people were walking around, screaming, and climbing the walls half-dressed. I learned later that Barton Hall was where the most seriously mentally ill patients were placed and that my mother was diagnosed with schizophrenia, a serious brain disorder that distorts the way a person thinks, acts, expresses emotions, perceives reality, and relates to others.[6] Once I entered Barton Hall, it was obvious my mother did not know who I was. I sat with her for an hour while she just rocked back and forth. Every now and then she stopped and looked at me as if asking, 'Who are you?' Then she started rocking again. She never spoke to me. She never said anything. It was a difficult time. It was not until I returned to the car and was riding back with my father that I faced the reality of my situation and said to myself, 'You don't have anybody. You can't count on your father. You can't depend on your mother; she can't help you. Whatever you are going to make of your life, you are going to have to do it yourself.' I maybe shed a few tears, or perhaps, none at all. I really do not remember crying. I mostly recall being dry-eyed and a little numb during the drive back to Chicago.[7]

Two cold, hard facts were undeniable to her at that point. Big Momma was dying and her father had lied about her mother. Iralee did not have a nerve condition but was seriously mentally ill and did not know who her daughter was. It seemed that her mother was lost. There was the additional difficult fact of living in a kitchenette apartment with an unsupportive, abusive father, his disagreeable girlfriend, and two sisters in no position to help. Contact with Little Jesse had abruptly ended. His mother had married and moved to Gary, Indiana with her husband who had adopted Little Jesse and changed his surname to Washington. Family was the vaguest concept it had ever been.

Reflecting on fourteen years of coping with an abundance of pain, loss, and family disruption, nothing seemed to signal things to come in her life. Audrey was sustained by a heartfelt assurance that "the Lord had her in His hands; that there was a divine purpose in her life," convictions she felt without question since she was four years old.

Setting her sights on future goals, Audrey began collecting materials on medical-related matters. Every article, anything discovered discussing medicine, medical schools, medical study, and physician careers, was carefully cut out, organized, and placed in a red scrapbook. One article that had a tremendous initial impact on her was a story in *Look* magazine featuring medical students at Tulane University. It included a photograph of two medical students holding a bone box, one of the tools commonly used to support instruction about the structure and function of the skeletal system. All the various bones in the body were contained inside a box for medical students to study. The magazine article gave her an introductory glimpse of what medical school was like.

Approaching senior year, Audrey contemplated the advantages of going back to Tougaloo to college where people knew her, were familiar with her reputation as a good student, and would probably give her a scholarship. She expected that returning to Tougaloo would probably make it easy for her to rent a room or secure another workable living arrangement. Going to college was not only mandatory for moving toward a medical career but a means to getting out of the house.

One of the positive distractions for her while growing up in Chicago was church. Church was a turning point for her in many ways. Surprisingly, Jesse was a regular churchgoing man who took her, Gwen, and Barbara to Tabernacle Baptist without waiver. He was an active member himself, serving as an usher, and wanted his daughters involved with church happenings. Reverend Louis Rawls, cousin to the famous singer with the same name, was head pastor at Tabernacle Baptist Church. Being a minister related to a celebrity brought a certain notoriety to the church. With no shortage of faithful members, Tabernacle was able to build a new sanctuary and designate the original space for young members, creating essentially their own church. The youth membership grew at a faster pace than the main congregation.

Audrey and Gwen sang in the young people's choir at Tabernacle. The choir travelled to perform in Evanston and other parts of the Chicago metropolitan area. The appearances gave them opportunities to experience communities they would not have likely been exposed to otherwise. The choir director, Mrs. Grace Burt Taylor, was addressed by everyone as Aunt Grace. She had a music studio in her home that Audrey often went to after school to practice songs selected for the upcoming Sunday. A native of Washington, DC, Mrs. Taylor had married a minister from Atlanta and lived there for several years before coming to the choir in Chicago. Mrs. Taylor developed a knowledge of and fondness for Spelman College while she was a resident in Atlanta and became an avid recruiter for the college.

When Audrey made a casual comment about returning to Mississippi to attend Tougaloo College, Mrs. Taylor was quick to respond: "Oh, no, you can't go to Tougaloo. You've got to go to Spelman." Audrey had not heard of Spelman College, and before she could state the fact, Mrs. Taylor added: "Oh, Mr. James would love to have your voice. Mr. James would love to have you in the Glee Club." Given the quality of Audrey's soprano voice, Mrs. Taylor was convinced she would excel in the music program as a vocalist. She was unaware of Audrey's plans to major in science to prepare for moving on to medical school. Mrs. Taylor encouraged Audrey to research and learn about Spelman, then instructed her to write a letter to Miss Florence Read (1886–1973), president of the college, expressing her interest in enrolling. Mrs. Taylor insisted on Audrey allowing her to proof the letter to the president before it was mailed.

Audrey followed every instruction given by "Aunt Grace." In the correspondence, she informed President Read of Mrs. Taylor's referral, shared information about her Mississippi and Chicago backgrounds, family situation, schools attended, grades and that she was graduating as the valedictorian at Wendell Phillips in a class of nearly three hundred. She concluded by asking for financial assistance.

President Reed's response was swift and positive. Audrey was admitted on a full-tuition scholarship with room and board. Overjoyed by the news, she interpreted the acceptance and offer as a divine gift—the important first step on her medical career journey. Mrs. Taylor then surprised her with a second "blessing," reiterating a promise made months earlier about a gift of her own, stating: "I'm going to give you a graduation present. I'm going to give you a trip to Atlanta to attend Spelman's commencement." True to her word, Mrs. Taylor made all the arrangements for Audrey to travel to Atlanta at the end of the school year.

Audrey took the train from Chicago to Atlanta, where she was picked up at the station and driven to Spelman's campus by a friend of Mrs. Taylor. Setting foot on Spelman's grounds was exciting enough, but the moment she entered Sisters Chapel, Audrey knew she was in the right place. She felt an immediate connection, an instant sense of home that she could not explain. The sensation heightened with the first sight of the graduating class marching into the Chapel in caps and gowns followed by the Glee Club in black dresses and white pearls, and the underclassmen in crisp white dresses. To her, it was perfect and more impressive than the processional witnessed at Tougaloo in terms of sheer numbers and regal essence. She thought, *Oh, this is great*! Then the swelling sound of the organ raised the level of magnificence even higher. It was the most amazing thing she ever heard. She recalled, "Sisters Chapel was majestic and powerful with a towering ceiling. Everything was on point. Everything moved right on time. At that moment, I knew Mrs. Taylor was right. Spelman was the place for me. The college was exactly what I needed to move ahead."

Audrey returned to Chicago, assured that she had been led in precisely the right direction and that Spelman was the perfect institution to initiate preparation for a medical career. That summer, she got a job, then put a few clothes together, bought a trunk, and was off to Atlanta. It was 1951.

CHAPTER 3

"Spelman College Saved My Life"

Traveling to college was an unforgettable journey for Audrey. The trip placed her on the career path she defended repeatedly during high school whenever it was suggested she should become a teacher, or when Jesse tried to persuade her to take typing to "be able to get a good job as a secretary." She remained firm, always insisting, "No, Daddy, I am not going to be a secretary. I am going to college and then I am going to medical school. I am going to be a doctor." Her comments clarified repeatedly that she knew her life's purpose.

The train ride included a stop in Nashville, Tennessee, where Mary Alice Lloyd, another incoming freshman headed to Spelman, boarded with her mother. As passengers in the rail car designated for Black riders, headed for the same destination, and having time to spare, the two became acquainted. Mary had a general notion of college life since her mother was housemother for the male dormitory at the American Baptist Theological Seminary (now American Baptist College) in Nashville. Audrey was openly optimistic and ready to take advantage of every opportunity available at Spelman. The two incoming freshmen arrived on campus together and ended up being roommates.

They were among the "eager and expectant group of freshmen that joined the Spelman family and inherited the ideals and traditions of the school." One of the city's elite African American colleges in the Atlanta University complex, and the nation's oldest and best-known liberal arts college for African American women, Spelman had trained female students for service and leadership in the Black community and beyond since 1881. The institution's success was mirrored in the history of alumnae such as aviator, nurse, and business pioneer Janet Bragg (1907–1993); barrier-breaking civil rights attorney Dovey Johnson Roundtree (1914–2018); prize-winning author Eva Rutland (1917–2012); and international opera star Mattiwilda Dobbs (1925–2015). Audrey set her sights on joining the legacy of Spelman women who excelled in medical science such as Dr. Georgia Rooks Dwelle (1884–1977)—the first Spelman graduate (1900) to attend medical school and established the first general hospital for Blacks in the state of Georgia (1920)—and Dr. Helen Elizabeth Nash (1921–2012), a 1941 Spelman graduate who broke racial and gender barriers in the medical field.

Audrey made good friends while settling in the freshman dorm and registering for classes. During the first week, she met Altona (Toni) Adelaide Johns (Anderson) (1935–2019), the oldest daughter of Reverend Vernon Napoleon Johns (1892–1965), a civil rights pioneer and pastor of Dexter Avenue Baptist Church in Montgomery, Alabama. She befriended Lydia Tate Walker (Whatley), whose mother was a Spelman alumna and father was a Morehouse graduate, and history major Amy Laura Irving (Richardson). When her popular roommate and secretary of the freshman class, Mary, did not return the second year, Audrey and Toni Johns became dormmates and roomed together for their remaining three years.

Majoring in biology, she opted for a double minor in chemistry and mathematics. Hitting the ground running academically, she registered for the most demanding courses available in both disciplines. She considered it was proper preparation for the rigorous medical school curriculum ahead. It became apparent to her during the first week of classes exactly how challenging the course load was. She had to work hard to stay on top of her studies, avoid distractions, and remain mindful that it was training for future leadership. She wanted to make the most of the four years.

Dr. Helen Tucker Albro (1898–1962) taught the freshman biology course. She had headed up the biology department since 1931. Audrey recognized right away how important the first-year course was. She explained: "As a science major, you had to pass freshman biology or risk doing the whole freshman year over. If you did not pass everything after being given a second chance, you could not remain at Spelman. In that respect, Dr. Albro was the de facto dean of the program."

When Audrey auditioned for the Glee Club, she realized Mrs. Taylor was right again. Willis Laurence James (1900–1966), chairman of the music department and director of the Spelman College Glee Club, was happy to have her. He took an immediate interest in her participation during the first year. Mr. James personally arranged voice lessons for her even though she was not a music major. The lessons were given in the hope that she would consider changing to the music program. She did not. However, it was an honor having Mr. James regard her voice so highly.

The group's reputation for choral excellence dated back to its inception in 1924. Pianist, organist, and concert violinist (William) Kemper Harold established the

Spelman College Glee Club, having previously founded the Morehouse College Glee Club in 1911. Harold directed music between the two colleges until he retired in 1953. Since 1933, he was assisted by his protégé, Mr. James, who held the position at Spelman for the remainder of his career.

Joyce Finch Johnson joined the music faculty at Spelman in 1953 and served as accompanying organist for the Glee Club. She was equally proficient on piano and, as official organist of the College, quickly became a reputable fixture for chapel, conferences, recitals, commencement, and numerous other campus programs, including the popular, highly acclaimed Holiday Concert. Since its inception in 1927 by President Florence M. Read (1886–1973), the two college choirs presented an annual joint Holiday Concert. The Christmas Carol Concert was initially held at elaborately decorated Sisters Chapel, the larger venue on the two campuses at the time. Singing to packed houses, the audiences came from throughout the South, typically arriving an hour early to guarantee they were able to get a seat. The filled-to-capacity performance every year marked the official opening of the holiday season for both colleges and generations of African American Atlantans.

While effectively lending its solemn ambience to countless worthy events, Sisters Chapel remained, first and foremost, the spiritual center of Spelman College. For Audrey, it was the sacred space that gave her a sense of home at initial contact; the place where she was transformed:

> The minute I walked into Sisters Chapel I knew I was in the right place, and that I was walking on hallowed ground. It was a miraculous thing. I thought, 'You just can't get any better than this.' It's the most majestic thing you can see; it's glorious with its towering ceilings, powerful organ, and precision. Everything moved right on time. It was perfect.

Sisters Chapel was where her spiritual needs were often met, where she heard inspirational speeches and witnessed great performances. Pretty much immediately, it claimed a special place in her heart.

Sisters Chapel was the site for graduations, Founders Day celebrations, convocations, concerts, theatrical performances, dance recitals, meetings, morning chapel, worship services, and any number of additional special college gatherings. Nationally and internationally renowned figures such as First Lady Eleanor Roosevelt (1884–1962), Dr. Mary McLeod Bethune (1875–1955), Dr. Robert Frost (1874–1963), Dr. William Edward Burghardt (W.E.B.) DuBois

(1868–1963), Dr. John Hope Franklin (1915–2009) and Dr. Howard Thurman (1899–1981) addressed students in Sisters Chapel. Performances were presented there by such acclaimed artists as Marian Anderson (1897–1993), Arturo Toscanini (1867–1957), Virgil Fox (1912–1980), and Paul Robeson (1898–1976).

Chapel services were held Monday through Friday mornings each week from 8 am to 8:30 am. Attendance was mandatory, and the doors closed promptly at 8 am. Everyone had an assigned seat by class, and attendance was taken. It was understood that arriving late meant being marked absent, and excessive absences could prevent you from graduating. Sunday vespers at 3 pm were also required.

Audrey was diligent when it came to Chapel requirements, but shared the sentiment of students who felt the social life at the college, in general, was too contained. Any number of activities—dances, art receptions, and sporting events like basketball and football—were enjoyed primarily by moving back and forth between campuses. Out-of-state students had limited contact with Atlanta proper. Atlanta was a city known for its Black middle class and elite that emerged despite disenfranchisement and the imposition of Jim Crow laws dating back to the 1910s. Most daughters of these families attended Spelman, and, along with others, enjoyed thriving social and cultural exchanges beyond the reach of on-campus students. At the time, on-campus students did not experience "Sweet Auburn" Avenue, which *Fortune* magazine described as "the richest Negro street in the world" in the 1950s, and the *Atlanta Journal-Constitution* considered to be the "epicenter of African American business acumen, excellence and innovation."[1] Only a choice few students ventured along Hunter Street (currently Martin Luther King Jr. Drive), to places such as Washington Park and Collier Heights. African Americans formed their own local amenities, not yet moving into neighborhoods that systematically kept them out, although the changing demographics and landscape of Atlanta would begin to manifest in the 1960s.

The grip of segregation on prevailing practices was affecting hubs like downtown, in spite of the anti-segregationist voice of the *Atlanta Constitution* editor and publisher, Ralph McGill (1898–1969), who wrote about the unconstitutionality of such behavior. The racial climate was a stern reminder to her that the city was in the South, and the cautionary measures enforced at the colleges were not only justified but necessary. Spelman campus students were issued a warning that it was wise for them to minimize travel to downtown or avoid doing so altogether.

When leaving campus, students were required to sign out and sign back in when they returned, which had to be no later than five o'clock. They had to be appropriately dressed, wearing heels, stockings, hats, and gloves, and had to travel in twos or more. Nearby West End Mall was within walking distance from campus and was the preferred shopping area. Stores on the mall carried a few supplies and personal items not obtainable on campus. The same off-campus rules applied. Like most students, the only feasible time for her to make an excursion to the mall was on Saturday afternoons. Morehouse students were subjected to similar routines and had to wear a shirt, tie, and jacket when they left campus.

On one of only two occasions when Audrey went downtown during her four years at Spelman, she was with a group of classmates that wanted to see the movie *The Robe* (1953) playing at the Fox Theatre, which was technically located to its north in midtown. African Americans were not allowed to enter through the front of the theater, being required to go down an alley on the side of the building, and up the fire escape to a balcony entrance.

Even though there was no pressing reason to go downtown, Audrey felt a certain way about it. While never speaking it out loud, at certain moments she thought to herself: *After all, I'm from Chicago... What do you mean I can't go downtown? Why do I have to wear heels and stockings and dress up to go downtown?* Years later, she understood the rationale. The rules were designed to keep Spelman women safe and Morehouse men away from potential serious problems: "That's the way it was in the 1950s across the South, even in Atlanta. It was worse in Mississippi. Tougaloo students seldom went into downtown Jackson. Everything they needed was on campus." Audrey complied, not wanting to risk losing her scholarship.

There was a bond between Spelman and Morehouse dating back to an official academic accord established between the two institutions, and resulting from a history of social engagement. Audrey began hearing stories of romantic possibilities between Spelman women and Morehouse men, upon arrival at the college; how some students placed the greater priority on building a relationship with a Morehouse student than reaping the educational benefits of attending the college. Some parents, according to grapevine legend, made great sacrifices to send their daughters to Spelman, with marriage to a Morehouse man as the main objective.

Audrey was fascinated with the leadership at Morehouse. President Dr. Benjamin E. Mays (1894–1984) was a rather soft-spoken, eloquent speaker about the dignity of all human beings and the incompatibility of expressed American democratic ideals with American social practice. As a major figure in Christian ministry and among the most articulate and outspoken critics of segregation in the nation before the active rise of the modern civil rights movement, Dr. Mays was a respected voice in the push for racial equity. He mentored a cadre of civil rights activists that included Martin Luther King, Jr. (1929–1968) and Julian Bond (1940–2015). Dr. Mays inspired students to excel in academics and life, and challenged them to become active participants in efforts to combat racial inequality methodically and with nonviolent resistance. His book, *The Negro's God: As Reflected in His Literature* (1938), outlined his liberation theology and explored portrayals of God in biblical, classical, political, and sociological literature. Further, he identified recurring themes that resonated with and contributed to many fundamentals of the prevailing culture of African Americans.

In frequent convocation addresses and special lectures, Dr. Mays clarified aspects of the Atlanta University Center's (AUC) motives for demanding strict compliance with dress and behavior codes on and away from campus. His explanations helped Audrey understand and appreciate how institutional policies were designed to combat stereotypes and dispel misinformation about African Americans and how the value of their college educated communities. She considered exposure to Dr. Mays to be among the highlights of her undergraduate life in the AUC.

In 1953, during the spring semester of Audrey's sophomore year, President Read announced her decision to retire. After serving as Spelman's fourth president for twenty-six years, Miss Read was set to conclude her presidency at the end of the academic year. Her administrative leadership was highlighted with accomplishments, including setting up the college endowment fund, forging affiliation agreement with Morehouse College and Atlanta University (which created the foundation for the AUC), obtaining Spelman's A-rating from the Southern Association of Colleges and Secondary Schools, and becoming an Association of American Universities institution. The physical plant expansion with the addition of Sisters Chapel, Trevor Arnett Library, Read Hall, Abby Aldrich Chadwick Hall, and establishment of the annual Spelman–Morehouse Christmas Carol Concert, with the initial concerts held in Sisters Chapel being among other significant developments.

On a personal level, Audrey could not forget the role Miss Read played in facilitating her being able to attend Spelman. The legacy established by Sophia B. Packard (1824–1891), co-founder and first president from 1881 until her death; Harriet Elizabeth Giles (1828–1909), co-founder and second president until 1909; and Lucy Hale Tapley (1857–1932), who presided over the college for seventeen years prior to Read's appointment, added to her belief in the unquestionable leadership ability of woman. Whatever speculation circulated regarding who would succeed Miss Read, the prevailing assumption on campus was that the tradition of female leadership would continue.

Surprisingly to the Spelman student body, Dr. Albert Edward Manley (1908–1997) was chosen as the incoming fifth president of the college. Being the son of Jamaican parents, he was sent to the US to live with relatives in North Carolina to go to elementary school. Association with Historically Black institutions dated back to his undergraduate study at Johnson C. Smith University in Charlotte, North Carolina (C'30). He later served as dean of North Carolina College (now North Carolina Central University), where he challenged students to "develop the ability to think creatively and carefully about ways to deal with social injustice."[2]

His appointment at Spelman gave Albert Edward Manley the distinction of being the first male and first African American president of the college. Described as a strong advocate for equality and education, he expressed belief in the capacity for excellence in leadership and achievement in women. In spite of his pro-female stance, the announcement of his appointment was met with opposition from students who felt strongly the position should continue to be held by a woman. Audrey was among the activists who led a student demonstration:

> We held a quiet protest, the type that Spelman women did in those days. Everyone wore gym sweats to class and to chapel in protest of Albert Manley coming. Some faculty members joined with us. But our efforts had no effect. He was confirmed and officially named president of the college in September 1953.

The ceremonial inauguration of the fifth president marked a new era in the history of Spelman College. Honorary board chairman and twenty-five-year board member Dr. Trevor Arnett (1870–1955) installed Dr. Albert Manley on Thursday, April 22, 1954, before the Board, students, faculty, and guests, including representatives from seventy colleges and universities from across the nation. Audrey participated in the ceremony as a member of the Glee Club, which performed a piece written by Mr. James specifically for the event, and heard a recital by tenor Roland Hayes (1887–1977) that drew an overflow crowd that gathered outside of Sisters Chapel and listened via loudspeakers.

Audrey, along with close classmates Altona Johns, Lydia Walker, and Amy Irving, arranged a meeting with the president soon after his installation "to tell him what he needed to know." Her three friends expressed concerns about matters such as visiting hours—how, for example, Morehouse students had to leave the campus by five o'clock, and Spelman students were not allowed to go on Morehouse's campus unless chaperoned, leading them to meet at the Atlanta University Library located between the two schools.

Audrey stated three issues firmly: "Number one, the chemistry courses at Spelman are weak. The courses were designed for home economics majors and are not strong enough for students, like myself, who are planning to go to medical school." She therefore, petitioned the president for permission to take chemistry classes at Morehouse College. She added:

> Number two, we have a rule that requires lights out at ten o'clock, which is enforced by the housemother. As a biology major with a double minor, all of the required lab courses and three jobs, I cannot afford the luxury of going to bed at ten o'clock. Because of my loaded schedule, my study time begins at ten o'clock most evenings, forcing me to resort to hiding in closets and bathrooms to study. These are measures I should not have to take because there should be an alternative place to study for students in my situation, or we should be allowed to stay up and study in our rooms. Third, there is a no card playing rule. No card games can be played on campus.

As someone who liked to play bridge, she argued there was "merit in allowing students to participate in an activity that was a common form of relaxation and interaction among women that was socially acceptable."

Voicing these issues formed the basis of her first face to face encounter with Dr. Albert Manley. The president responded positively to her requests. She received permission to take chemistry classes at Morehouse. The lights out at ten o'clock rule was adjusted to allow extended time for study when necessary, and a study area was set up in each dormitory. A game room was added even though bridge, at the time, was being trumped by bid whist, which was becoming increasingly more popular. In a very short while, there was almost always a game going on in the room. Although she had lobbied for it, Audrey had very few opportunities to play, but was among the numerous students who dropped by the game room between classes for a quick check on who was playing and how a game was going.

Audrey had a wonderful experience at Spelman. She was exposed to people, opportunities, and learning situations that she probably would not have enjoyed otherwise. She was even grateful for her three jobs. The two with the biology laboratory were on Saturday mornings involving taking inventory, making sure everything needed for the upcoming class was set up properly, and caring for specimens such as frogs, cats, or whatever else was pertinent. Her third obligation was in the music department where she took roll for the Glee Club. Mr. James had a rule that if you did not attend rehearsal, you could not sing at the next performance. His rule was strictly enforced. He would sometimes say to a student, "You weren't at the last rehearsal. I don't remember you." Then he would double-check with Audrey asking, "Forbes, was she here?" She received no money in hand for the jobs. Funds were used to offset the cost of her room and board, a common means of support when she was a student.

By the end of junior year, she had completed or was enrolled in science courses needed for medical school preparation with an excellent performance record. She was scheduled to take the MCAT (Medical College Admission Test) within the necessary timeline, had assisted well in the biology lab, and completed all other requirements. Looking toward medical school, there were two institutions that accepted Black applicants in the 1950s: Meharry Medical College in Nashville, Tennessee, and Howard University in Washington, DC. Other programs were possibilities on rare occasions. She followed the customary course of action, like most of her Morehouse contemporaries, and applied to Meharry and Howard. She sent a packet to the University of Illinois on the outside, hoping she might get accepted by chance. Being a resident of the state, she thought there was a slim possibility of getting in if the school was amenable to bringing in qualified African American applicants.

Meharry wasted no time. They responded in a week, stating bluntly, "We want you." Acceptance was contingent on successful completion of courses in progress and remittance of a fifty-dollar deposit. Fulfilling course requirements was a given. Securing the upfront funds was not so easy, but she managed, thrilled by the idea of gaining acceptance into medical school. Bottom line, the wait was swiftly over. There was no need to beat on anyone else's door.

At that juncture, seeing her Morehouse classmates gain entry into medical school was important to her, and she was led to repeatedly ask them, "Have you heard?" and pleased to learn when each one received an acceptance letter. It turned out that the majority were headed to Howard with at least one going to Meharry.

Senior year was a busy time filled with numerous class activities along with finalizing academic requirements. She continued to participate in Biology Club and Glee Club events, was winner of the "Know Your Spelman" Quiz for a third consecutive year and was elected a senior class officer along with Eleanor

Williams, Evelyn Cooper, Mildred Ealy, and Barbara Yancey. Audrey worked as subscription editor for the yearbook alongside "talented, hardworking young women who exemplified the unity, cooperation and success" of the class, with her closest friends, editor Lydia Walker, typist Amy Irving, and assistant editor Altona Johns among them. The other seniors were editor Claudia Dell Finger, literary editor Evelyn Belmaize Cooper, business manager Reba Wilson assisted by Mary Lola Whatley, Flora Mae King, and Frankie Ruth Hamilton; art editors Betty Ruth Taylor, Billy Joyce Douglas, and Yvonne Parks Hunt; feature editor Elsie Mildred Mallory; and typists Helen Anita Taylor, Alice Rosetta Zuker, and Jean Claudette Byrdsong.

Approaching the final weeks of undergraduate study, Audrey reflected on memorable aspects of her student life at Spelman. She recalled how her first friendship was initiated with another incoming student in a segregated rail car on the way to campus; how it grew while they shared a freshman dorm. All the things learned and discipline instilled from her lab responsibilities, demanding course load and long days that gave her a fleeting, but nonetheless candid glimpse of the rigors of medical school life was seen as invaluable. The lifelong relationships established with Morehouse chemistry classmates gave her a deep sense of camaraderie. Glee Club participation gave her a voice and an outlet like no other, along with its adventures and the additional opportunity to become further disciplined and to enjoy working with others toward a unified goal. She was able to squeeze in a precious few bridge games that provided her with much-needed down time and casual student fellowship.

Described by yearbook contributors as "skinny, inquisitive, loves ice cream and bridge, sings incessantly, energetic and effervescent…freckles," she had her own overview of the graduating class which she outlined in terms of the depth of diversity of talent, social acceptance, generosity, leadership roles, and academic successes, concluding optimistically: "Many experiences remain in store for us. We hope that the spirit of our past will inspire greater triumphs in the future."

Graduation was a critical milestone. Earning a biology degree gave her a profound sense of accomplishment. Just as no family member had visited her during the four years of study, none of them came to her graduation. She was a realist who understood that Iralee was confined to a hospital room, Jesse was preoccupied with outside relationships, and Gwen and Barbara were dealing with their own problems. As such, she celebrated with the lifelong friends with whom she shared the college journey, her Spelman sisters. Their fellowship and warm farewells softened what might otherwise have been a painful memory of aloneness at a pivotal moment of accomplishment.

Later that same day, Monday, the sixth of June, Audrey gathered her belongings and left Atlanta the same way she arrived—by train, and filled with optimism, excitement, and anticipation of things to come. It was 1955.

CHAPTER 4

Tragedy and Triumph: The Meharry Years

Nashville was well known as "Music City USA" when Audrey arrived. Home to the Grand Ole Opry, publishing houses, and recording studios situated along Music Row, the capital city was a different place from the African American perspective.[1] It was where HBCUs Meharry Medical College, Fisk University, Tennessee State University, and American Baptist College were founded. These institutions advanced career, character-building, and cultural traditions, including the Jubilee singers, debate teams, and world-class athletes. It was the home of WLAC, Talkradio 98.3, one of the first 50,000 watt radio stations to air music by Black artists. Inspired by Black college students who, in 1946, insisted on hearing a different sound and supplied the station with a stack of records, WLAC became one of the channels on the forefront of introducing R&B music to widespread audiences.

Nashville was also the base for civil rights activist Kelly Miller Smith, Sr. (1920–1984), pastor of First Baptist Church (Capitol Hill) from 1951 until his death, president of the Nashville National Association for the Advancement of Colored People (NAACP), founder and president of the Nashville Christian Leadership Conference, and a founding board member of the National Urban League. Smith, Sr., would later become assistant dean at the Vanderbilt University Divinity School and the school's first African American faculty member.[2]

Audrey entered this general milieu but remained focused on the fact that being in Nashville marked the beginning of her medical training and she was eager to get started. As one of eight in the first freshman class to officially include women, she soon recognized the extent to which her Morehouse exposure, although highly beneficial, had not sufficiently prepared her for the male-oriented culture prevalent at Meharry.[3] Studying under the strictness of Dr. Henry McBay at Morehouse had paid off academically. She knew that succeeding in his demanding courses conditioned her for anything she might encounter in future study, but she had no idea how challenging the social mandate ahead would be.

The situation at Meharry was candidly clear from the onset. The college was devoutly male oriented. Women had no option other than to adjust. There was no prearranged housing, dining hall access, or consideration given to accommodations for female students. More emphatically, it struck her bluntly that, given the nature of the school's history, there was no sisterhood. Finding herself at a place that was diametrically opposite from the college life previously known, Audrey managed to remain motivated by concentrating on her ultimate goal of learning everything well and completing all requirements for the sake of getting out.

She arrived in Nashville early enough in August before classes began to look for an affordable place to live within walking distance of campus. As was typical with HBCUs, most amenities were in relatively close proximity to the college. In this case, almost everything was within a circle—the school, boarding houses, and popular beer establishment at the corner of Jefferson Street and 17th. The club near Meharry was where students gathered for beer and social interaction on Friday nights. With segregation still the order of the day, and the availability of goods and services being met close by, there was no need to go downtown, even if it had been a safe, viable option.

There did not appear to be a relationship between HBCUs in Nashville similar to that witnessed in Atlanta, even though Fisk University was across the street from Meharry, and Tennessee State University was nearby. A formal relationship existed between the affiliated institutions in Atlanta, as well as their collective relationship with the city's broad-based African American leadership. The situation was preached about regularly from the pulpits in Black Atlanta. On the other hand, Meharry had its own appeal, most notably its contributions in healthcare fields, and the contention that some young ladies who attended Fisk might get a Meharry man (marry a successful doctor), reminiscent of the scenario at Spelman regarding Morehouse men. Although it was casually noted, Audrey had no real opinion on the matter, remaining faithful to her academic objectives and appreciating the rich legacy of all of the institutions.

Meharry was impressive. The college was organized in 1876 to provide medical training to former slaves, teaching the initial eleven students in the basement of Clark Memorial United Methodist Church. Within ten years, Meharry added programs for nurses and dentists and distinguished itself as the medical institution for African Americans. The college grew from being the Medical Department of Central Tennessee College to become the largest and second oldest medical school for African Americans in the nation. Meharry was the first medical school in the South offering four-year preparation for students, and the largest private historically Black institution in the US whose sole purpose was to educate healthcare professionals and scientists.[4] By the time Audrey entered, Meharry was graduating annually approximately 40 percent of all African American doctors and dentists in the country, and had a motto that aligned with her personal values—"Dedicated to the worship of God through service to man."

Dr. Harold Dadford West, Sr. (1904–1974) had taken office in 1952 as the medical school's first African American president. Dr. West worked his way through the ranks of associate professor of physiological chemistry, professor, and department chair at Meharry. His vision for the institution included curricula and infrastructure expansion, faculty and staff growth and the development, and demonstrative reiteration of commitment to the College heritage of "preparing students to serve with honor, dedication, and distinction all over the world."[5] As an entering freshman during Dr. West's third year of leadership, Audrey did not over-analyze the timing of her admittance or lose sight of the opportune course of events that unfolded before her. She was cautiously enthusiastic about the next four years, a quasi-reticence that proved justified, as the transition from undergraduate to medical school turned out to be an even greater challenge than she originally imagined.

Finding suitable housing took its toll, time-wise and otherwise. She ended up renting one of four rooms that the property owner had added to the rear of her boarding house. Rent covered use of a shared bath and access to the refrigerator. Audrey rarely ate there, opting to eat at neighborhood places despite having a limited food budget. Only male students who lived in the dorms were permitted to eat in the dining hall on campus. There were no restaurants to go to. Families opened up their homes to feed many Meharry students. Upperclassmen and other off-campus students such as Audrey relied on neighborhood homeowners for food. Students could purchase meal tickets from homeowners for thirty dollars a month, which paid for two meals a day—breakfast and dinner. Sunday meals were really special. The homes were set up to seat ten students in the dining room and ten on a closed-in porch. Typically, two men served the meals and both tables were usually full.

The academic and social climate on campus was apparent early on. It was an atmosphere that was far from ideal from the standpoint of women. Rather than being discouraged, it triggered the beginning of another cause in her—advocacy for women in medical science.

Freshman year was the hardest, even though she managed to establish a workable routine, form close friendships, and become part of a tightly knit study group. One friend was Clarice Delores Wills (Reid) from Birmingham, Alabama. Her parents and paternal grandmother were educators, and she, along with two older brothers, became science majors. Clarice had a photographic memory and graduated with honors in biology from Talladega College in 1952. After earning a degree in medical technology at Meharry two years later, she spent a year in Cincinnati, Ohio, working as a medical technician at the Jewish Hospital, and met, then married an ambitious young lawyer, Arthur J. Reid, Jr. When Clarice returned to Nashville in the fall of 1953 to enter the medical program, she joined her brother, Noel Wills who was a second year student at Meharry's Medical College. Audrey and Clarice formed a close friendship, sometimes studying together.

They shared a penchant for bridge that resulted in them pairing up to play cards most Friday nights. Bridge was a major relaxation outlet for Audrey that placed her in a socially different group from those who ventured into the streets looking for things to do. She was not the typical college social being, never seeing herself doing much more than studying and playing bridge: "I was so skinny; not aware that guys ever looked at me. One thing is for sure, men were not following me to the bridge table."[6] To her, bridge was practical. It costs essentially no money to sit down with a deck of cards and engage in an unassuming exchange in a game that was a good mental exercise. Bridge formed the extent of Audrey's social life and was a serious avocation for Clarice, who came from a family of bridge players.

When Clarice relocated to Ohio with her husband two years later and continued study at the University of Cincinnati College of Medicine, they remained good friends. Audrey was already in a study group with two Spelman alumnae that entered Meharry with her. Lola Jean Scott had been a biology major and history minor, finishing number one in their class. Wilmotine Brenda Jackson graduated in biology ahead of them in 1951, and worked as a physical therapist for four years in Atlanta before entering Meharry. The three bonded effortlessly, even though their interaction at Spelman had been little to none. Audrey had very limited prior contact with Lola Jean, an Atlanta native and day student who returned home when her classes at Spelman ended every day and, therefore, was not around when those who lived on campus, mostly out-of-state students, socialized, studied, and got to know each other. Audrey did not become acquainted with her until senior year, and while they may have casually discussed interest in medical school, she had no idea Lola Jean would be attending Meharry. She had no previous interaction with Wilmotine, who graduated from Spelman in the spring prior to Audrey entering as a freshman in the fall. Wilmotine returned to Meharry as a medical student on the strong suggestion of a doctor friend practicing in Atlanta.

Audrey considered meeting Clarice, Lola Jean, and Wilmotine providence, feeling blessed to have good friends. The study group gave her a sense of camaraderie and belonging, and was an overall source of stability for her in the midst of difficult adjustments near campus. The members of the group supported one another, and since Wilmotine had certain advantages—an apartment, new car, money, and a supportive boyfriend who was also in the group—her home became the usual place for study sessions. It was not unusual for them to study until two and three o'clock in the morning, compelling Audrey on those occasions to catch a few hours of sleep on a couch or on the floor before rushing off to her rented room to shower, dress, and make it to her 8 am biochemistry class.

Life in the classroom and around campus in general was customarily unpleasant. Female students were frequently the targets of inappropriate comments, off-color jokes, innuendos, and subtle insulting remarks. Certain professors channeled lecture statements and instructional procedures down insensitive gender paths that were blatantly intended to cause embarrassment or to make female students uncomfortable in class. Withstanding this type of treatment was a relatively routine part of Audrey's medical college life. She avoided internalizing its negative impact by mentally processing the incidents as stamina and endurance training, situations that prepared her to deal with almost anything that might be confronted professionally in the future. She rarely took the time to bring it up with the others, or assess her general feelings about medical school, having decided that no matter what happened, she would finish and get out. There was also realization of the likelihood that the same treatment prompted her friends to develop coping mechanisms of their own. As such, she "kept her nose to the grindstone, studied hard, passed exams, and learned to survive from crisis to crisis."[7]

Racially motivated episodes unrelated to school also had to be endured when off campus Audrey gave the following account of a travel incidence with a group of male Meharry students:

By now I'm in a situation where there are a few male students with cars. It was common to take a trip home for the holidays. Once there was this gentleman at school who was going to drive from Nashville to Gary, Indiana, to be with his wife and children. He was looking for other students who needed or wanted a ride there so they could help pay for gas. Instead of trying to get a train, if you could get a ride home that was even better. As it turned out, his car was loaded up; there were three people in the front and three in the back. He was driving along legally, headed to Gary. When we crossed the state line into southern Indiana, a police officer drove suddenly out of the woods with his lights flashing and stopped us. He said to the driver, "I want to see your driver's license. You're speeding." Of course, the driver wasn't. We all knew he was driving under the speed limit.

Everybody was quiet; did not say anything; did not speak back. The men in the car were like wooden soldiers. After receiving the license and glancing at it, the officer said, "Well, that's going to be sixty dollars." I didn't know if we had sixty dollars between us. We had pooled money to pay for the gas. So, I did not know about sixty dollars. Then, the officer said, "Well, come on and follow me." It was dangerous; awfully scary. But he had his red light going and he told us to follow him, so the driver did. He had no choice. He drove into this little opening and there was a house with a section on the back that looked as if it had been added, and there was a United States flag on a flagpole in front of the area. We went inside and a judge came out in his bathrobe. It was obvious he had been asleep. But there we were, the six of us. Quiet and not knowing what was about to happen. After being told by the officer that the driver was speeding, the judge wanted to collect the sixty dollars. We put together what we had, trying to see if it added up to sixty dollars. By that point, I was traumatized. I was the most afraid of all of us and think it showed. When we put together the amount we had, someone said, "Well, Judge, we've only got forty-eight dollars." He answered, "Well, I'll take what you've got." He took it, and let us go. That was 1957. He was just shaking us down to get money. That's all it was.[8]

She added,

> Things could have been worse. It was a very dangerous situation. I was the only woman, and wondered if my being there possibly made a difference; kept them from doing something worse. We knew how it was, traveling through southern Indiana, southern Illinois, southern Missouri, and all those type places. We knew where the traps were. You took the chance to get where you were going and hoped that you would get through without a problem. Anything could have happened. We could have been killed.[9]

As if life at Meharry did not present enough of its own challenges, she had to overcome the sudden, unimaginable string of personal losses that consumed her years in medical school. Sophomore year turned out to be the most devastating. By that time, she and Lola Jean had become best friends. They shared an attic space that had been converted into a make-shift apartment in a home where they were provided with homecooked meals that they ate with the family. They were as close as friends could be. Audrey knew that Lola Jean had gotten engaged to her boyfriend in Atlanta before coming to Meharry. As far as she could tell, the boyfriend was faithful, attentive, and always sending lavish gifts as token reminders of his affection, gifts that Audrey believed were probably beyond his financial means. Unfortunately for him, Lola Jean met, dated, and fell in love with another medical student at Meharry. The relationship escalated to the point that Lola Jean decided to break off her engagement in order to focus on being with the man she loved in Nashville. Audrey, out of concern, advised her repeatedly throughout the courtship to tell her fiancé that she was seeing someone else. Lola Jean chose to wait, insisting she would take care of it when she went home.

At the end of the academic year, they left for their respective hometowns, expecting to return in the fall to start junior year together. Audrey headed to Chicago, while Wilmotine and Lola Jean departed for Atlanta. Everything changed dramatically that weekend. Once home, Lola Jean apparently followed her planned course of action as discussed with Audrey and told her fiancé about seeing another man and her decision to cancel their wedding plans. It was a dire situation that did not turn out the way Lola Jean had hoped. The result was a tragic one. Audrey received the news over a Saturday night phone call from Wilmotine, informing her that Lola Jean was murdered by her boyfriend. Upon learning her justification for breaking off their engagement, her boyfriend apparently returned to her home the next day (June 4, 1957), shot, and killed her, then turned the gun on himself. Sadly, her mother returned home to discover both bodies.

The heartbreaking news of Lola Jean's murder was far beyond anything Audrey could have imagined. It was incomprehensible. Hearing devastating words through the phone in the voice of one close friend about the death of another was surreal. The emotional impact was tremendous, personally and financially. She had to delay finding a much-needed summer job to cover expenses for the next school year and borrow train fare to travel to Atlanta for Lola Jean's funeral. It was a lonely, tough trip, but she had to do it. They had been like family, and as difficult as the ordeal was for her personally, her heart ached more for Lola Jean's mother. It was important to be there for her as well.

Moving forward in the fall was a daunting endeavor. One thing was certain, she could not return to the attic unit that had been shared with Lola Jean just a few months earlier. The mere thought of being there alone was its own nightmare. Fortunately, before she had the chance to consider alternatives, Wilmotine came to her rescue, offering her the extra bedroom in her apartment. It was the perfect solution, insuring Audrey of physical and emotional companionship during the difficult adjustment at Meharry. She, nevertheless, had to brace herself for the return trip. She made it back, but returned deeply wounded. The shock and pain of Lola Jean's death were still fresh. There were tearful moments when thoughts of Lola Jean unexpectedly surfaced, or during quiet times of reflection when she felt how sorely her friend was missed. For the duration of her time in Nashville, Audrey slept with the lights on in her room every night.

Wilmotine was a generous person from a prominent Atlanta family. She appeared to have an ideal life with no financial worries. Her bills were paid by a well-established physician friend in Atlanta and received an allowance from her parents that insured there was always plenty of food and liquor at her home. With so many positive things going on in her life, it saddened Audrey to witness her friend essentially drinking her way through Meharry. Wilmotine and her boyfriend spent the better part of Friday nights and Saturdays consuming alcohol. They sobered up on Sundays to have clear heads for classes at the beginning of the week. To Audrey, Wilmotine seemed to have a constitutional problem with drinking. She wondered if the doctor friend who came to town from time to time noticed her condition on his visits. Audrey could not tell since, on those occasions, she left the apartment and busied herself elsewhere.

As her concerns about Wilmotine grew, a horrible tragedy struck again toward the conclusion of her fourth year. During finals week, as everyone in the senior class was preoccupied with completing exams and making preparations for graduation and their subsequent departure home, she was stunned by a second tragic event. Days before joining a family of prominent doctors in North Carolina, a promising female classmate was involved in a love triangle that had fatal consequences.

The young woman was the sole female who socialized in a circle of male students that included her married boyfriend. The couple studied together and was essentially inseparable outside of the classroom for four years. She was presumably led to believe that after graduation, the boyfriend would divorce his wife and they would be married. To the girlfriend's surprise and dismay, news from his home shattered her hopes. Once her boyfriend learned that his wife was pregnant with twins, he decided not to file for divorce, to end the affair, and resume married life with his family. The situation was, apparently, too difficult for the girlfriend to face. Tragically, she snapped. While the two were together in her apartment near campus, she apparently fatally shot him, then got into her car, and drove off a cliff. Later, it was revealed that she had prepared a will that left everything she owned to the boyfriend's widow.

She and Audrey did not form a close friendship, but given the small number of women in the medical program, and the two of them having entered Meharry together, they shared a general sense of awareness and a mutual regard for one another.

Audrey was jolted by the news, compounded by the heavy weight of concern she carried for Wilmotine. For the two years, she and Wilmotine roomed together. Audrey never offered unsolicited advice or was inclined to judge, but her commitment to silence wore thin as she watched her close friend's talent being diminished under the pressures of a lethal romance. When Wilmotine's boyfriend left Nashville immediately after graduation and returned to Memphis without giving a thought to their relationship or her emotional well-being, Audrey watched her friend surrender her life more and more to alcohol.

The tragic death of her best friend, murder-suicide of an admired classmate, and essential loss of a second dear friend to drinking cast a huge cloud over what would have otherwise been a ceremonious commencement. All accomplishments notwithstanding, Audrey's Meharry experience was defined as much by tragedy and pain as preparation for medical practice. She considered the Meharry years the worst time in her life.[10]

One bright light was meeting Dr. Georgia Bone Mitchell, a Meharry alumna who finished the previous year and successfully completed an internship at St. Mary's Mercy Hospital in Gary, Indiana. St. Mary's Mercy Hospital officials were so impressed with Dr. Mitchell's performance, they sent her to recruit more Meharry graduates as interns. A Nashville native who excelled while a student at Meharry, Dr. Mitchell was an effective ambassador for the institution's program and emphasized the bottom-line benefits. She pointed out to Audrey: "This is a good internship program. It pays well. The work is hard, but they are looking for a minority person. They are looking for it." There was the added advantage of Gary being less than thirty miles from Chicago, which was still Audrey's home. She was sold.

Commencement was bittersweet but victorious. She met her goal. The medical degree was in hand. From that moment on, she was Dr. Audrey Forbes, and about to embark on her first professional position in the medical field. It was the spring of 1959.

CHAPTER 5

Gary, Indiana: The Medical Career Begins

Everything changed the minute Dr. Forbes left Nashville. The title of medical doctor gave her a newfound visibility that she concluded, "transformed her from being an unwanted urchin sitting by the fire into someone no one wanted to kick around anymore."[1] Bound by train to Gary, Indiana, she arrived July first, during a time when the city was still thriving due to its huge steel industry and when its demographic trend was gradually shifting.

Dr. Forbes reported to St. Mary's Mercy Hospital confident and well prepared to apply the training received at Meharry. The internship offered her the initial opportunity to examine, diagnose, and provide healthcare services to patients. She was, less conspicuously, on a trajectory that would facilitate accomplishing another mission—blazing a trail for other African Americans in the field in general, and Black women in particular. Her unassuming point of beginning in that regard was at Gary's St. Mary's Mercy Hospital.

Founded by the Sisters of St. Francis in 1908, the facility that began with a small staff, four modest residential units connected by modest walkways evolved over time to become St. Mary's Mercy Hospital, a 500-bed medical center that for decades was one of Gary's premiere healthcare institutions.[2] When Dr. Forbes, along with friend and fellow Meharry graduate Dr. Charles Relerford, were recruited as interns, St. Mary's Mercy Hospital historically had multiple departments—surgery, obstetrics, X-ray, and physiotherapy—but specialized in obstetrics and pediatric cases. The hospital also ran a school of nursing in the building.[3]

Dr. Forbes was part of a four-member team, which meant she was on call every fourth night. Her compensation included a free, fully furnished apartment across the street from the hospital, two hundred and forty dollars a month, and twenty-four-hour access to an abundance of food from the well-stocked refrigerator and pantry in the interns' quarters. It was a relatively generous financial arrangement, since the monetary amount earned exceeded the fifty to one hundred dollars typically received at other hospitals, and the generous food provisions freed her of the need to grocery shop. She emphasized that "whether it was 2 am, midnight, or six o'clock in the morning, it didn't matter, you could just go by the interns' quarters and get what you needed or what you wanted." However, work was as demanding as she anticipated, adding: "Sitting back with my feet up and watching TV in my apartment during off time was countered by the pressing demands of being on duty. That's when they got their money's worth."[4] Another plus factor was having Dr. Relerford and his family housed across the hall from her unit, which gave her a sense of family while in Gary.

The extent of Dr. Forbes' preparedness and competency was put to task in a very short period of time. She was contacted one evening by obstetrics and informed about a somewhat perplexing case. The nurse on duty impressed her as being experienced and knowledgeable of women in labor and delivery comparable to any doctor. Dr. Forbes noted, "She may not have been able to pass a formal medical test or written exam, but she knew all about pregnant women."[5] Once Dr. Forbes was on the floor, the nurse told her in no uncertain terms, "I don't know what is wrong with this patient, but she is not in labor." The patient had been admitted from the emergency room because her doctor, a well-established physician in Gary who was either unwilling or unable to come and administer an examination, had simply said, "Well, I can't get over there right now; just admit her." It was a typical response. Male physicians in private practice who used St. Mary's Mercy Hospital relied heavily on interns to perform certain tasks, including situations like this one. This meant the woman arrived on the floor without having been seen by her doctor.

White doctors were just beginning to care for Black patients at the time. The doctor in this case, being one of the city's best-known and highly regarded gynecologists, had arranged for a Black female patient to come through the emergency room. She was admitted close to midnight. The nurse, questioning why the woman should be admitted since she was not in labor, confessed that her initial inclination was to send the patient home. However, abiding by the doctor's instruction, and given the severity of the woman's complaint of abdominal pain, she thought it was best to ask Dr. Forbes to come and see her. After an examination, Dr. Forbes agreed that the woman was not in labor, being equally convinced her complaints were not imaginary. When the admitting doctor was contacted, he instructed her to "get a psychiatric consult." Dr. Forbes noted that, more often than not, when a White doctor reached the point where he wanted a psychiatric consult on a Black female patient under such circumstances, he had missed the diagnosis. It was an easy thing for someone like him to imply "it must be psychiatric," with her not being in labor but complaining of pain, the assumption being there was nothing physically wrong with her. "Get a psychiatric consult" was the standard response.

Dr. Forbes noticed the young woman had been given high levels of Demerol and it was not fazing her. After examining the patient and taking a history, she called the lab to the floor and ordered a sickle cell prep on the patient. Within a brief amount of time, the test results came back positive. Considering sickle cell anemia as a possible explanation for a woman's symptoms in such a scenario was emphasized during her training at Meharry. Given the cultural differences and lack of exposure to conditions of Black female patients on the part of White doctors who were just beginning to administer care to them, sickle cell disease was not something they were inclined to commonly consider. The tendency was underscored further by the fact that sickle cell impacts African Americans at disproportionate rates.

Dr. Forbes discovered the patient had hemoglobin sickle cell (SC) disease, the second most common type of sickle cell disorder but, unlike SS, where the anemia was less severe, the patient does not get in trouble often until they are pregnant, when the demand for blood from the fetus causes the cells to sickle.[6] Retrieval of the patient's history provided additional information. She was aware that patients with such diagnoses typically had a history of reported arthritis as children. While children do not have arthritis, in certain parts of rural areas, especially in the south, a child suffering with joint pain often had the areas rubbed with alcohol and treated as arthritis when, in reality, it was sickle cell. Misdiagnoses of Black patients occurred for years because not enough was known about sickle cell disease to identify that a child had the condition or that a pregnant woman was in crisis. Moreover, if the woman is late in her pregnancy, such as the eighth month, the baby draws all the blood and the mother's cells sickle, as was the case with the patient Dr. Forbes diagnosed at St. Mary's Mercy Hospital.

Successful handling of the patient's dilemma established her as the go-to person for difficult situations at the hospital. Directives to "call Dr. Forbes; she'll take care of it" became standard practice among most hospital staff. It was a practice perpetrated, in her assessment, by the divinely ordered courses of events that caused her to be at the facility and on call at the precise moment when a sickle cell patient arrived in distress. It was probably the first case of that type to come through the hospital's emergency room. Dr. Forbes' typical response to praise and expressions of gratitude were simply, "Well, thank Meharry for that."

On another occasion, when she was called to the medical ward, Dr. Forbes found the attending nurse in hysterics—trembling uncontrollably and appearing to be emotionally falling apart. Commenting on the condition of the patient, she was summoned to see, the nurse exclaimed, "Oh, she's a diabetic, Doc. She's a diabetic. She's going to go into a coma. She's going to die; she's going to die. You've got to do something quick, quick, quick. Here, I've got the insulin ready for you." The nurse had a large syringe of insulin prepared to give to the patient. In an attempt to calm the nurse down, Dr. Forbes asked, "Well, is she that bad off? Are you sure? Let me see the chart." Based on the information reviewed on the chart, Dr. Forbes concluded the patient should not be having any trouble; and, noticing that she had received eighty units of insulin at seven o'clock, there was no way she needed more insulin at that time.

Dr. Forbes examined the patient, then instructed the nurse, "Get me a syringe of 20 cc of 50 percent glucose." The nurse responded, "You're going to kill her. She's already a diabetic. She's in a coma. She needs insulin. You need to give her some insulin." Dr. Forbes was unfamiliar with this particular nurse, but stated to her firmly, "Did you hear what I said? I said get me a syringe of fifty percent glucose and get it now." When the nurse adamantly refused to do so, Dr. Forbes told her, "Okay. Then sit down. Get out of my way." It was a scenario that Dr. Forbes as a Black physician would become all too familiar with—giving a direct order to a White nurse regarding the treatment of a White patient, and having the nurse feel entitled not to obey it. To confirm this was the case, she asked the nurse specifically, "Are you refusing to do what I asked you to do?" The nurse responded, "Yes. I'm not going to do it." Taking matters into her own hands, Dr. Forbes said, "Okay." She went to the locked medicine cabinet, retrieved the 50 percent glucose, filled the syringe, and returned to infuse the patient. As expected, the patient came around immediately and began talking, asking, "What happened?" Dr. Forbes informed her, "It was your insulin. It just kicked in."

Not letting the incident go, she wrote an official report of the events leading up to the patient's proper treatment, reprimanding the nurse for insubordinate behavior that could have put the patient at risk. She stated, "The assisting nurse refused to take a doctor's order. She refused to do what I specifically asked her to do. If I had given this patient the insulin she prepared, I would have killed her. The patient was in insulin shock." Dr. Forbes noted that in such a situation, where there is a diabetic patient in a coma, you give them insulin to bring the sugar down. Having done that, you do not need to administer more. You have thrown them into insulin shock. The eighty units given to the patient had reacted. It was necessary to bring her back. Once that is done, the patient does not just slumber back. They wake up immediately alert and curious. As a result of her report, the nurse was released.

Dr. Forbes, self-described as "a skinny little Black woman all of 99 lb," came on her service call not expecting to have to deal with insubordination but, in the interest of providing the best patient care, was fully prepared to do so. News of her actions resonated quickly throughout the hospital, with nursing staff, particularly, taking note. She made a name for herself again. This time she was respected even more for her no-nonsense attentiveness to patients, and her willingness to deal with any nurse who questioned her authority as a doctor because she was not a White man. Having established her zero tolerance for such behavior, things went relatively smoothly for the remainder of her time at St. Mary's Mercy Hospital. Her cases were often chosen for the hospital's grand rounds and highlighted in discussions of procedures based on her effectiveness.

When the end of the internship was on the horizon, deciding on a specialty became an important order of business. She chose pediatrics. Experiences during her junior-senior year clerking and her intern year at St. Mary's Mercy Hospital helped her realize she liked working with babies. She developed a special interest in small children, partly because they were the most vulnerable patients. She had become a pretty good diagnostician, a much-needed talent when addressing the medical needs of infants. She noted,

> Babies are a challenge in one way because they cannot talk. They cannot tell you what is wrong. You have to read the signs of a baby's illness, whether it's their eyes, skin, heart rate, lungs or how they're holding their limbs. You have to take into account everything you physically see, X-rays, and lab work to get the proper diagnosis.

The next important decision was where to apply for residency training. It was a big move, and her selection had to be finalized before July first, the deadline to be out of the apartment at St. Mary's Mercy Hospital to make room for the next intern. The amenable places in the country where an African American could get training as a pediatric resident were Meharry's George W. Hubbard Hospital in Nashville, Howard University Hospital in Washington, DC, Homer G. Phillips

Hospital in St. Louis, Mercy-Douglass Hospital in Philadelphia, and Provident Hospital in Chicago.[7] Dr. Forbes was well aware of them all.

Provident Hospital, established in 1891, was the first African American owned and operated hospital in America. Mercy-Douglass Hospital dated back to 1895 and had the first Black nursing school in Philadelphia. Homer G. Phillips Hospital was the sole medical facility for African Americans in St. Louis when it opened in 1937 (and would continue in that capacity until it closed in 1979). Howard University Hospital, initially Freedmen's Hospital, was established in 1862 to serve the medical needs of African Americans who migrated to the district during the civil war. Hubbard Hospital began serving the African American community in 1931. These were the Black hospitals that were solvent enough to have residency training programs and were the schools that produced nearly all of the Black doctors who had specialized up to that time.[8]

The social climate in America was shifting. The nation was noticeably on the verge of undergoing the unrest and social change that would largely define the 1960s Civil Rights Movement. Dr. Forbes was aware that "while more conservative institutions continued to resist letting Blacks attend, some hospitals with more liberal leanings were beginning to let a trinkle in, accepting one or two African American residents to be able to say that they were not segregated and, therefore, not discriminating." In spite of these overtures, HBCU hospitals remained the places Black applicants relied on. "Between them, you knew you could get a Residency."

While contemplating residency options, her classmate, neighbor and friend, Dr. Relerford, was making arrangements to return to Griffin, Georgia, immediately at the end of the internship for urgent family reasons. When she learned his wife developed cancer during pregnancy, with her condition advancing to a stage where chemotherapy was advisable, her heart went out to him. She subsequently learned Mrs. Releford gave birth to a healthy baby, but did not survive. It triggered an emotional throwback to the sad times Dr. Forbes went through during her Meharry days. She understood why Dr. Releford decided to set up private practice in his hometown to better care for his newborn rather than going through a residency.

Dr. Forbes was leaning toward hospitals in St. Louis and Chicago. St. Louis was appealing because her former choir director, whose support dated back to her high school days, was living there. This made Homer G. Phillips Hospital appealing. Provident was a viable option since she still had family in Chicago, even though her sisters, father and mother were pretty spread out. Further,

Dr. Lela Bell Freeman, a Spelman graduate, who wrote one of her recommendation letters to Meharry, had finished Provident and would be supportive. Dr. Forbes was actually familiar with people who had attended each of their schools. At one point, the question was put before her, "Why don't you try Cook County?" She was quick to respond, "They are not going to take me. They have never had any Black residents, so they are not about to take me." When the argument was made that she had nothing to lose, so why not apply to Cook County anyway, she insisted on dismissing the idea, certain that Cook County Hospital had not changed.

Chicago's Mercy Hospital was another matter. It was one place she believed might be conditioned for change, commenting, "I'm not going to be so brash as to try Cook County, but Mercy might take me." Their pediatric program was run by Dr. Joseph Christiansen, someone she heard speak while a student at Meharry. Dr. Forbes recalled he was "a very nice, charming, and handsome man." More importantly, she believed it was a good possibility that Mercy might not have completed their residency selections. On the chance that they had not, she submitted the proper paperwork to Mercy Hospital and also applied to Homer G. Phillips. Shortly afterward, she received a call from Dr. Christiansen at Mercy. He told her:

> Dr. Forbes, I have received your application package. As a matter of fact, I have it in my hand right now. We have filled our quota for Mercy training, but I know they still have openings at Cook County. Do you mind if I send your application over to Cook County?

She said, "Of course, I don't mind." At the same time, her thoughts were that he was wasting his time, concluding, *There is no way in the world Cook County is going to take a Black person, and a woman at that.*

A few days later, she received a call from a representative at Cook County Hospital wanting to schedule an interview. Totally surprised, she thought, *I'm not in yet. But they did say come for an interview.* Making the appointment required careful planning since she was still completing the internship in Gary. The good news was by then she had a car, a stark difference from when she approached fulfilling all study requirements at Meharry. At that time, there was a free week between the end of exams and graduation.

In that case, during the interim, every man in her class went home to buy a car, and drove back to Nashville in a large Oldsmobile, Pontiac, or Cadillac. She was the only graduate to leave without a vehicle, relying on the train for transportation home to Chicago, then, in July, to Gary. Once at St. Mary's Mercy Hospital, she went to a local car dealership and bought a car. She indicated:

> That was 1959 and I purchased a 1958 floor model, a Rambler. I paid fifty dollars down and my car note was fifty dollars a month. But at least I had wheels. When I drove to Cook County Hospital for the interview, it seemed to go well, although, I left uncertain if, or to what degree, they were impressed.[9]

Apparently, they were. Dr. Forbes was notified of her acceptance. She became the first African American female resident at Chicago's Cook County Hospital and only the second African American overall. It was 1960.

CHAPTER 6

Making History at Cook County Hospital

Going to Cook County Hospital as a resident was a professional breakthrough Dr. Forbes had not envisioned. Implications of the achievement were augmented by the fact that she did not personally pursue the residency; Dr. Christensen facilitated it. However, it was her reputation and performance that ultimately opened the mammoth door that had been virtually closed to African Americans in the past. Her acceptance was a welcomed development, placing her not only on a list of firsts but putting her back in Chicago, where family matters could, conceivably, be more readily attended to when needed.

At the time, the patient population at Cook County Hospital was approximately 95 percent Black and 5 percent other groups. The hospital staff was 100 percent White, representing people trained at international institutions and from the best White schools in America. Her earlier skepticism about securing a position was based on this reality, even though, theoretically, the demographic divide made the fact that Cook County Hospital had not taken an African American woman before, and only one Black male in the history of the hospital, incredible.

To her mind, the course of events leading to her receipt of a positive response could only be explained in terms of the miraculous. She believed the experiences and opportunities offered would augment the training she received at Meharry Medical College and first-hand practice at St. Mary's Mercy Hospital. The timing of her acceptance in the program turned out to be significant, occurring during the advent of the 1960s civil rights movement. Activism was noticeably on the rise in populous cities such as Chicago, and Dr. Forbes was not oblivious to the potential role healthcare facilities may have to play as the push for equity in America continued to escalate.

Cook County Hospital was a choice location for training at the time, being considered one of the best programs in the country. The work was demanding. They saw 1,000 patients per day. As such, in light of its reputation, Cook County

Hospital attracted residents from prestigious higher education institutions across the US and from medical institutions in friendly nations internationally. Her circle of colleagues included residents from Ethiopia, Mexico City, and Portugal. Despite being the sole African American, the youngest, and doing noticeably impressive work, she did not give a second thought to the trailblazing nature of her presence or outstanding performance. Instead, she remained focused on the day-to-day tasks necessary to administer quality care to patients.

Self-described as someone "who was moving too fast to worry about a record,"[1] Dr. Forbes exercised the same intensity of determination, commitment, and attentiveness that led to her success as a student at Spelman and Meharry, and extraordinary intern at St. Mary's Mercy Hospital. She explained:

> At Cook County, I remained in the moment, doing the best job possible while dealing with all of the issues that confronted a Black doctor working in a White setting on the other side of town from Provident Hospital. One thing I did know; being the first, I could not fail. Failure was not an option because I had to do what was best for patients and I had to establish something for other Spelman women to come.[2]

Six months into her first residency year, she was summoned to an administrative staff meeting. Hospital administrator Dr. Rowine Hayes Brown (1913–1999) told her, "Dr. Forbes, you have been given the most difficult assignments each month, and on each occasion, you have done an outstanding job." She listened intently, not sure where the comments were headed, having given little thought to the degree of difficulty of her assigned work relative to other residents. She knew the most challenging times of the year were referred to as the two diarrhea seasons. In this case, it meant October 1961 and June 1962, with October having been the worst. It was a time when the hospital experienced a near epidemic of gastrointestinal disease in babies, and the mortality rate on the diarrhea ward was usually in the neighborhood of 30–35 percent. She had been assigned to the Diarrhea Service Ward 16, where they admitted twelve to fifteen babies every day, making it necessary to discharge that number each day.

When asked: "Do you know what your mortality rate was?" Dr. Forbes admitted, "No, I did not calculate it; I just recall we lost one infant that was transferred to the service in the middle of the night from the premature ward to avoid getting a diarrhea spread there. Unfortunately, the baby died within the hour."

At that point she was told: "Well, your mortality rate was less than one half of a percent." This meant that she and her staff had not lost a baby that came into the service for diarrhea treatment. Among those patients, all were treated and sent home. In the final analysis, she was informed by the medical director, "You are going to be named chief resident. And the reason why I have asked you here this morning is because you get a choice of what service you want to have the next three months because in October you will be named chief resident."[3]

It was the most coveted position to achieve in a residency training program. As chief resident in pediatrics, she had twenty senior residents, twenty junior residents, and fifteen interns on the service. Dr. Forbes explained:

> Cook County was a five-hundred-bed hospital for children. If there was a question regarding what to do about a baby or infant—if a doctor could not figure out the diagnosis, or get in a vein, or decide whether a child should be admitted—they called the chief resident to come down, do a consult, and advise them what to do. The chief resident is part of the training staff for the junior and senior residents, and in charge of the hospital. If something goes wrong—oxygen tanks, tents, X-rays—the chief resident is contacted to either fix whatever is wrong or get someone else to do it.[4]

No one ever asked how she managed to achieve a perfect survival rate with the babies admitted for treatment during such a critical month. Following her natural instincts as well as training, she paid attention to commonalities in symptoms and took into account cultural factors. She tactfully identified the most urgent cases, while indicating to the mothers of others that the needs of their children were important. She instructed them to do things that helped and sustained their babies until they could be seen. Her professionalism did not mask an understated compassion for them as infants or patients in need of help.

Thinking about a personal childhood experience, Dr. Forbes offered this account:

> I remember when, as a child in Mississippi, I had an experience once with a White physician. At that time White physicians rarely treated Black patients and there were only two Black physicians in Jackson. I had a horrible rash, which required a Dermatology consult. The Black medical doctor sent me to a White dermatologist for the consult. I remember passing the waiting room, a large room full of White patients. There was a small room in the back of the clinic after you passed this huge, very nice waiting area. It was about the size of a closet and

> had four folding chairs inside. I was the only patient waiting. I sat in one chair, my mother in another. As a Black patient, you waited until the doctor finished with all of his White patients and then you would be seen. That process was my earliest personal exposure to medical treatment for Black people. I realized that was the way it was across the South.[5]

Memory of that experience remained fixed in her mind while growing up in Chicago, where the same pattern of behavior was prevalent. For the most part, Black patients went to Black doctors on the South Side, and White patients went to White doctors on the North Side. Reflecting on the similarity, she realized just how parallel the entire healthcare situations were. She became well aware of the fact that Blacks who needed medical attention and were poor did not have insurance and did not have money came to Cook County Hospital. The situation was the same because despite the considerable number of major teaching hospitals in Chicago, none of the others were seeing Black patients at that time. Being the county facility, it was even the place that the police would transport people to in paddy wagons for care.

There were always patients waiting to be seen at Cook County Hospital. The normal wait time in pediatrics was three hours. If the waiting time exceeded three hours, there would be trouble because patients would die in the waiting room before they could be seen by a doctor. Prior to her becoming a resident, it was not unusual for there to be a mother holding a baby wrapped up in a blanket to assume everything was basically okay with the infant and the baby would pass away. If it is a diarrhea patient, they were assigned to that ward, even though they never got to the floor. That was the typical scenario in the Children's Hospital.

Dr. Forbes made a habit of walking through the admitting room at seven o'clock each morning on her way to the Diarrhea Service Ward, and asking the clerk at the desk about the wait time. Depending on the response, she would determine at that moment the kind of intervention needed. If the clerk informed her that they were running behind four or five hours—it very seldom got to be more than three hours, though it could—her reaction was usually, "Well, that is too bad; we're going to have trouble all day." She proceeded to speak to each of the mothers, instructing them to uncover their babies, since they usually brought them wrapped in a blanket, thinking they were helping them. She told them, "I want to see your baby's face. I want you to take the top off of your baby's bottle and smell the milk. If that milk is sour"—which it was most of the time—"don't give the baby any more of that milk. That will only make them sicker and make things worse."[6]

She noticed that most of the mothers were very young. Many were fifteen, sixteen, and seventeen years old. Dr. Manley concluded that, in all likelihood, their grandmothers, who normally were the people in their lives who gave them sound advice, were still in the South, not with them in Chicago. She examined their babies one by one, then instructed them: "If I tell you to come with me, then gather all of your things, tell the clerk at the front desk to scratch your name off the list, then follow me. I am going to hold the elevator until you get there."[7]

She typically came onto her floor accompanied by seven or eight mothers carrying infants determined to be staring at death's door. "Based on how they were breathing, their fontanels, whether they were sucking and the look of their eyes were clues to their critical state."[8] Once the infants that were most at risk were on the floor, everything was set up to treat them right away. Standing orders were for 50 cc of blood plasma, which she kept in small bags in the refrigerator followed by Ringer's lactate to weight. Dr. Forbes prioritized taking steps to save an infant's life first over attending to paperwork. On too many occasions, she observed medical students recording long patient histories and making sure the information was correct and written up properly while the mother waited for her baby to be taken care of. She reversed the process: content that once a baby's weight was determined and initial care given, there was plenty of time to get history later. Such departures from traditional procedures contributed to the ultimate saving of infants' lives.

Dr. Forbes achieved various successes over the initial several months at Cook County Children's Hospital, but it was clear she was named chief resident primarily because of her performance in October on the diarrhea ward. Serving as chief resident changed the trajectory of her training and future plans. It was a difficult and demanding job, being essentially on call twenty-four seven. She might be summoned at two o'clock in the morning if there was a problem or someone came in with a condition that the on-duty staff could not diagnose or was unable to determine what was wrong. It was her responsibility to attend to those and other matters to ensure problems did not reach Dr. Brown and the medical director, Dr. Joseph Greengard. Describing herself as "the first Johnny on the case," she gave specific instructions to residents not to call either of them before calling her, adding, "If I cannot handle it, then I know what to do."[9]

As chief resident, Dr. Forbes answered emergency calls from the office of Mayor Richard J. Daley (1902–1976), attended to City Hall requests from municipal government individuals seeking care for a patient, or responded to someone from the north, west side or other location in the city wanting children examined for any number of reasons, one example being in order for them to attend summer camp. She was the point person for all types of medical-related courtesy services that Cook County provided for the mayor's office. The frequency and nature of the interactions made her intimately aware of the close connection between public health and politics—the politics of medicine.

Managing residents was another important function. On those occasions when residents and interns gathered in the early hours of the morning to talk, which Dr. Manley referred to as jam sessions, she quickly reminded them:

> If you are on duty, you need to get back to work. We have no time to talk. If we are more than three hours behind on wait time, we will have dead babies on the tables. You were not sent here to talk. Get to your rooms and see your patients.

She continued:

> They always responded 'Yes ma'am,' and went back to work. They did not say anything else, grumble, or complain. It was an interesting situation. There I was, only twenty-seven years old, the only Black doctor on staff and the first Black woman ever in the position, telling these White doctors what they needed to do, and they did it. But what I knew, and they had to keep in mind, was the fact that people would die if we were not on duty. Cook County Hospital was seeing 1,000 patients every day, every 24 hours. No. We could not stop. We could not have a break. Patients depended on us.[10]

The historic significance of her appointment did not go unnoticed by the local media, including the *Chicago Tribune*. In a newspaper article published shortly after her promotion, Cook County Children's Hospital warden (superintendent) Frederick A. Hertwig praised her superior work when confirming her as chief resident. Dr. Joseph Greengard, chief of the pediatric staff and director of pediatric education, emphasized how, in addition to her medical ability, she demonstrated leadership qualities conducive to effective oversight of residents and interns. It was emphasized that at age twenty-seven, she was the youngest person ever named chief resident at that point in addition to the distinction as the first woman and only second African American. News of her recognition had farther-reaching implications than she imagined. Many people in the healthcare community took notice, along with others whose interest she had not imagined.

The biggest surprise came from her undergraduate alma mater. She recounted:

> One day I was sitting in the dining hall of the dormitory at the hospital in Karl A. Meyer Hall. It was an eight-story building housing residents and interns named for the distinguished surgeon who served Cook County Hospital for 53 years as an administrator, surgeon, teacher, and politician. Meyer Hall was a facility where everything was self-contained. A basketball court, swimming pool, and other recreational things were on the fourth floor. The cafeteria was on the second floor. On this particular day, the article appeared in the *Chicago Tribune*. Several people came by the table where I was seated, wished me well, and offered congratulations.
>
> Then suddenly, I heard my name over the PA system: "Paging Dr. Forbes. Paging Dr. Forbes." I rushed to the phone thinking, *What now? What can't they do? What do they need me for now?* Instead of the call coming from a member of the hospital staff, it turned out to be Mrs. Ernestine Brazeal, director of alumnae affairs at Spelman College. She said, "I understand you are in the paper today, and I should wish you congratulations." Those of us who went to Spelman always marveled at the fact that Mrs. Brazeal knew everything about alumnae. But I could not help but wonder how in the world she knew about the article. She was in Atlanta. How could she possibly know the piece on me was in the paper that just came out that day? The question was soon answered when Mrs. Brazeal added, "Dr. Manley is in Chicago. He is doing fundraising for UNCF [the United Negro College Fund]. He is at the Palmer House and he wants you to call him." I was both flattered and amazed.[11]

Dr. Forbes had a form of hero worship for people in leadership at Spelman, and thought, *Dr. Manley, oh, my goodness. This is big time*. Then, she immediately called him.

Speaking with Dr. Albert Manley, the conversation ended with her inviting the president to visit Cook County Hospital, which he accepted. The next day, he joined her for lunch at the Karl Meyer Resident Hall. President Manley was introduced to Dr. Greengard and Dr. Brown, and was given a tour of the hospital by Dr. Forbes. She outlined her responsibilities in surgery, radiology, cardiology, diarrhea, and other services. Dr. Manley was impressed with the extent of her duties and obligations and the professional levels on which she apparently executed them. At the conclusion of his visit, he was impressed even more by comments from Dr. Greengard, who encouraged Dr. Manley to "send us more student doctors like Dr. Forbes."[12]

She subsequently drove President Manley to O'Hare airport in her little green Rambler to catch his flight back to Atlanta, thinking that was the end of it. Time would tell a different story.

The nature and scope of her attention to nutrition-related health issues in infants while chief resident was noticed by science professionals at Abbott Laboratories. The American multinational medical devices and healthcare company was headquartered in Abbott Park, Illinois, thirty-seven miles north northwest of Chicago. They wanted to test a formula—Similac with iron—on one thousand small babies, Black babies preferably. Representatives from Abbott Laboratories approached Dr. Greengard and the Chicago Board of Health about conducting the clinical study at their facility. They selected Dr. Forbes. She believed there was no better place than Cook County Hospital for the research, since the nursery easily handled the desired number of babies each month. Abbott Laboratories wanted one person to do the work to minimize error and hoped to have results as soon as possible. Due to her reputation, Dr. Forbes struck them as the ideal physician for the research.

The company was eager to confirm the effectiveness of the product and get it to market. Dr. Forbes was interested in having a viable supplement accessible to mothers that could improve survival rates and quality of life for their babies. In the process, their mutual objective was to ensure the product solved the common problem of anemia in infants that were exclusively formula-fed who usually had low iron anemia.

Dr. Forbes clarified the nature of concerns from her perspective.

> At the time at Cook County Hospital, it was not unusual to have babies brought in with seizures and convulsions. In such cases, the first thing to do medically was to check their iron and sugar levels. Milk anemia was a threat in babies. This resulted from mothers having allowed their infants to have the bottle too long; and their babies were not fed enough solid foods like spinach, eggs and other sources of nutrients when they needed it. Drinking only milk, they ended up with low iron content. They sometimes developed seizures and were often overweight. They were large babies but lacked proper nutrition.[13]

It took her a year to complete the clinical research. She personally monitored every baby that was started on the iron supplement through the completion of the process. Dr. Forbes needed healthy babies to start on the formula, and therefore selected newborns that were thoroughly examined to make sure there were no underlying problems. The babies were brought back in six weeks for her to measure their iron levels, tested by the Chicago Board of Health. "Rather than waiting for babies to get sick, you start them off on the Similac with iron and avoid the illness altogether. You do not have occurrences of 'milk anemia.'"[14] Her successful clinical research of iron-fortified Similac facilitated the market availability of the formula, which benefited infant feeding needs.

In late 1962, when the end of her year as chief resident was eminent, Dr. Greengard and Dr. Ira Rosenthal, a member of the pediatric faculty at the University of Illinois and attending consultant at Cook County, made a special request. They informed her: "We want you to do something for us. The National Institutes of Health (NIH) has never awarded a fellowship to an African American physician and we want to use you as a test case to get them to make that kind of award."[15] It was another shocking and amazing moment that she did not see coming. As she contemplated the idea, the doctors elaborated: "They have never given a training grant to a Black candidate. We want you to apply so that we can break the ice."

She weighed the potential consequences on her personal life carefully and then concluded that the impact would likely be minimal, since her only responsibility beyond taking care of herself was her mother. By this time, Iralee was living with her brother (uncle). The facts were clear. She was young enough, not married, had no children, and was not tied down, so to speak, unlike many of her colleagues who had family obligations. She agreed to do it, and prepared her application for an NIH fellowship. In the back of her mind, Dr. Forbes wondered about other possible motivations should she receive the fellowship. She wondered if they might want to convince her to remain at Cook County Hospital and join the University faculty. She dismissed the likelihood of that motive because they did not pay anything; therefore, she could not afford to stay there indefinitely. However, she realized that, should things work out in her favor, it would probably open the door at NIH for other African Americans.

Dr. Forbes was awarded a fellowship in newborn physiology at the University of Illinois. Her preceptor was Dr. Marvin Cornblath. In addition to breaking the ice at NIH, receipt of the award made her the first African American faculty member at the university. Having been unfamiliar with NIH prior to becoming an applicant, and not knowing the agency-awarded fellowships, much less their history of not including African American candidates, she did not anticipate the impact her fellowship would have on Cook County Children's Hospital and future NIH training programs. She arranged to fill the time between the conclusion of her residency and the start of her fellowship as a special resident in order to spend a month each in hematology, cardiology, and neonatology, areas of interest that were not pursued earlier due to her quick advance to chief resident.

Meanwhile, she was the topic of another conversation in Atlanta. Dr. Albert Manley was in the position to recommend Spelman women for various career opportunities, one being with Operation Crossroads Africa (OCA). Founded and directed by Dr. James Herman Robinson, OCA was a US-based, private voluntary organization that sponsored cross-cultural exchanges and small-scale service projects in Africa. Dr. Robinson was seeking a doctor to head up a medical team for an upcoming program in West Africa. President Manley highly recommended Dr. Forbes for the job. It turned out to be another extraordinary career opportunity from a source with which she was totally unfamiliar. Having never heard of OCA, being already committed to conduct research, and teach at the University of Illinois, and having interests in other matters, the likelihood of her compliance with Dr. Robinson's request seemed slim. However, after closer examination of the program's mission, needs, and requirements, such as the cadre of twenty-five or thirty units that translated into Robinson's selection and training of five to ten people to go at a time, she accepted.

The assignment was to serve as the lead physician heading up a team of nurses and dieticians at an outpost in Enugu, Nigeria in West Africa. This added to an already full plate of commitments, which, most urgently, included completion of all residency obligations at the hospital and preparations to meet commitments as an NIH fellow. Once the additional obligation was made, Dr. Forbes negotiated an agreement with Dr. Cornblath to delay the start of the fellowship three months (until October) in order to participate in the Crossroads program. Dr. Forbes stressed that it was something she definitely wanted to do. Dr. Cornblath complied with the request, wanting her to have the experience. She was delighted, seeing the OCA offer as a once-in-a-lifetime opportunity.

Her acceptance strengthened the chain of information transmitted to Spelman. Everything she did from then on was picked up by the college, largely due to her open communication with President Albert Manley and Mrs. Sally McAlpin, chair of the Spelman College Board of Trustees. Her commitment to opening doors, paving paths, and accentuating what was possible for Black women in medicine and science deepened, especially in terms of motivating other Spelman women to go into the fields.

Dr. Forbes attended OCA training in New York along with her medical team. It was the first group of medical personnel for Crossroads Africa to go to Nigeria, and her first trip outside the US. They flew from New York to Dakar, Senegal, where they deplaned for a few hours. Although the time spent there was relatively short—far less than a day—she made good use of it in an effort to get a sense of the culture before continuing on to Abidjan, Ivory Coast. Hopes of having a brief look around Accra, Ghana, were thwarted when President Kwame Nkrumah refused to allow anyone in the country, so they pressed forward and landed in Lagos, Nigeria. From Lagos, the group proceeded to visit the University of Ibadan located 128 kilometers (80 miles) northeast of Lagos. The University of Ibadan had among its many units a College of Medicine, Institute of Child Health, and Center for Child Adolescent and Mental Health. It was one of the most prestigious universities in Nigeria. They next visited Kano, the second largest city in the country after Lagos and a major route of the trans-Saharan trade. With Kano located in the northern region, the trip required a two-day train ride, the most reasonable travel option since flying was not feasible and driving to Kano was not an alternative because roads in certain places were impassable.

Enugu was their destination, the secessionist state that would become the site of the Biafran Civil War with Nigeria between July 1967 and January 1970. The conflict erupted four years after Dr. Forbes and the medical team had completed their tour. She recalled a different political atmosphere at the time of her assignment:

> When we were there it was very peaceful. The country was beautiful. It was oil and diamond rich. The British exited around 1960 after Nigeria gained independence. As things happened there later, I have some idea of the ways they came about, knowing how situations were before. For example, I remember being in Kano, the capital, where there were large numbers of Muslim people. I remember how they were, as a rule, extremely tall like the Congolese-American basketball hall-of-famer Dikembe Mutombo. He would not stand out there. His height was typical.[16]

What she referenced was the tension that existed between Muslims and Christian Igbos that resulted in Igbo people fleeing to the Eastern Region in large numbers. The conflict did not surprise her years later. She discerned the roots of its beginning even though it was not something witnessed during her assignment.

Transitioning to the three-month work assignment involved adapting to the location and living situation in 1963. It was a smooth yet rapid undertaking. Based at Enugu General Hospital, Dr. Forbes provided full-time hands-on patient care, supervised the medical team, and directed observations of major medical facilities including the University of Ibadan and University of Nsukka (officially the University of Nigeria at Nsukka, UNN, a federal university in Nsukka, Enugu State, in the eastern part of Nigeria), as well as in Kano, Calabar, Kaduna, and Onitsha.

She worked with two female doctors from England, at the hospital. Interaction with them was informative, reminding her of the prominence of women in the medical field in other parts of the world. Awareness of the typically different situation in the US remained on her mind throughout her career.

Dr. Forbes got to know the particular area where she was based like the back of her hand very quickly. In addition to making regular rounds to facilities in the program, she took carefully planned road trips every weekend with her driver. She was comfortable living in the area and felt perfectly safe in the house, leaving windows open all night and sometimes sleeping on the porch. A full-time housekeeper maintained the residence, which contributed to making the house a place of relaxation and reflection.

At work, the program went smoothly, the impact of their presence being positive and them enjoying the benefits of a well-run, informative detail. At the same time, Dr. Forbes was not blind-sided to the long-term residual effects of colonization and foreign control on such nations after independence was achieved. She pointed out:

> It was unbelievable. But what happened was the case with so many of the countries that were dominated by European powers. It happened in Jamaica. I lived to see that, too. Wonderful place, beautiful weather, British rule, everything was working. Things were drastically different the minute they abruptly pulled out, which is how most of them did it. They just picked up and left. When, for example, the telephones went out, there was no one there to fix them. It was really awful. I have a deeper understanding of the African and Caribbean stories of what happened because of it.[17]

Dr. Forbes fulfilled all commitments in Africa and returned to the US on August 28, 1963. Her destination was Washington, DC. Flying into the capital, the timing was perfect from a historical perspective. Her flight, in the midst of its landing pattern, flew over the National Mall while the March on

Washington for Jobs and Freedom was underway. The aerial view captured the 250,000-plus demonstrators gathered around the Washington Monument, along both sides of the expansive, tree-lined Lincoln Memorial Reflecting Pool, and in front of the Lincoln Memorial itself. It turned out that the plane passed over during the precise minutes when Dr. Martin Luther King, Jr., was giving his iconic "I Have a Dream" speech. The scene was so impactful that it served as a firm reminder to her of all the work that needed to be done, the unprecedented accomplishments that needed to be made, and obstacles that needed to be removed or overcome to make a way for others, especially Spelman women.

Upon her return to Chicago, the next two years were devoted to her NIH fellowship as neonatology research associate at the University of Illinois School of Medicine. Her emphasis was newborn physiology under the direction of Dr. Marvin Cornblath. From 1963 to 1965, Dr. Forbes engaged in clinical research on health issues and diseases in newborns, premature infants, and low-birth weight babies. She taught clinical procedures to residents and interns, and oversaw patient care in the newborn and premature nurseries, follow-up clinics, and the Juvenile Diabetes Clinic.

She was the first observer on a twin study where the smaller infant had hypoglycemia. It typified the situation where twins in the uterus vied for nutrients from the mother through the vascular system. The twins were rarely the same weight—occasionally being identical but not always. In cases of inequitable size differences, the smaller twin is prone to develop hypoglycemia, which is low blood sugar that affects the brain, causes convulsions, and leads to other health problems. Studying blood sugar and low blood sugars in infants and children, and the impact on their mental faculties and growth was the primary emphasis of the research. Their findings were published in various medical journals, with Dr. Forbes listed among the authors.

Aware of her continued contributions in medicine, and being an alumna, President Albert Manley invited Dr. Forbes to join the Spelman College Board of Trustees. She was flattered, but initially hesitant to accept out of concern that it may be unwise to commit to such a responsibility at that juncture. There was already so much to do. The president assured her that demands on her time would not be too imposing since the board convened only twice a year, in the fall and spring. He suggested that any input she provided would make a meaningful contribution to the board's service to Spelman. After careful contemplation, she accepted.

Completing the NIH fellowship, she gave serious thought to private practice rather than pursuing employment with a hospital or health care system. She felt enough was enough, that it was time to get out of public health and get her feet wet in the real world. When she shared her thoughts, Dr. Greengard was the one discouraging voice. He did not like the idea of her going in that direction, and told her candidly: "You have too much to offer. You can do more for people outside than you can in private practice. But if you really believe you have to go, then go; but I do not think you will find it fulfilling."[18] Everyone else held silent, more or less having taken it for granted that once she finished training, the next step would be to go into private practice. Dr. Greengard, on the other hand, believed her passion was elsewhere. He insisted: "You are not going to be satisfied. You can do much more for your people if you are at County Hospital or someplace like that than if you are out there...Now, you think about that."[19] Dr. Forbes considered the possibility that he might be right but was not sure, and felt strongly it was something she had to discover for herself. She concluded that the only way to find out was by doing it—going into private practice. It was 1965.

CHAPTER 7

Private to Public Practice

Dr. Forbes had the professional and public demeanor of a woman who was all work and no play. It appeared on the surface as if she had no personal social life of any real consequence. To the contrary, she had caught the serious eye of an Intern on service with her at Cook County Hospital, Dr. Robert (Bob) Smith, whose overtures eventually got her attention. Dr. Smith's personality and demeanor earned him the reputation as "the classy Southern gentlemen who always sent her flowers." After a year-plus courtship as they completed their respective obligations to the hospital and Dr. Manley met all commitments to Cook County and the University of Illinois, Dr. Smith proposed. Her acceptance of his marriage proposal coincided with the decision to venture into private practice in the medical office of Dr. Larry Keith.

She and Dr. Smith discovered they had more in common than being in medicine, in Chicago and at Cook County Hospital at the same time. Both were natives of Jackson, Mississippi, had several mutual acquaintances, were familiar with many of the same places, liked many similar things and had personal histories with Tougaloo, Mississippi. Dr. Forbes spent time around the college campus while growing there, and Dr. Smith had completed undergraduate work at Tougaloo College before attending Howard University Medical School where some of her Morehouse classmates had studied.

As the newlyweds settled in their recently purchased two-story home, Dr. Forbes joined Dr. Keith at his well-established family practice located on the west side of the city. Her husband soon returned to Mississippi to fulfill a state obligation there. It was a common occurrence when Dr. Smith entered medical college for governments in the south to pay African Americans to leave their home state and study at an HBCU. Those governments covered full tuition costs at institutions such as Meharry and Howard rather than allow Black students to enter their state schools. Once their study was completed, they owed the state a designated term of service, typically two years. Dr. Smith had acquired his medical degree under such an arrangement with the state of Mississippi and went back to Jackson at the end of his internship at Cook County Hospital for that purpose. He was expected to return to the hospital once the obligation was met to become a Resident in OB/GYN. In the interim, they traveled back and forth intermittently to spend time together.

Dr. Keith's medical office was across town from Dr. Forbes' residence. With expressway construction just underway as a future option, she made the difficult surface-route commute from their South Side area home to work on the west side every weekday for two years. One evening she left the office headed to a house call. While waiting at a red light, she was rear-ended by a woman who was driving drunk. Seat belts were not mandatory in automobiles at that time, and the impact thrust her body up out of the seat causing her head to slam into the roof of the car. When everything was presumed to be resolved at the accident scene, Dr. Forbes continued on her way and then went home.

Trouble struck the next morning when she tried to get out of bed and could not move. At first, she was unable to even raise her head off the pillow. She eventually managed to make it to the emergency room at Mount Sinai Hospital, where it was determined that she had a whiplash and concussion. The injuries resulted in a ten-day hospital stay. Dr. Smith rushed to Chicago to check on her, and after a few days, with her concurrence, he returned to Mississippi before her release.

In the final analysis, she considered the accident another act of divine intervention. The hospital stay not only gave her sufficient time to physically heal, it provided a period of peace, quiet, and reflection. It gave her enough solitude to clear her mind of the busyness and pressures of daily routines, and to assess her life personally and professionally. She knew change was inevitable but appreciated having the opportunity to pause and think:

> I realized I had been working so hard, putting in such long hours and going through the necessary motions with my career that I did not really stop to think about what I was doing otherwise. For two years, Bob and I had a commuter marriage. That was not ideal. While I was working in private practice in Chicago he was practicing in Jackson. It took the accident for me to slow down long enough to see I was on the wrong page and had to do something to correct the situation.[1]

Dr. Smith's family practice in Jackson turned out to be so lucrative that he decided to rescind the residency at Cook County Hospital and remain in Mississippi.

He tried to persuade Dr. Forbes to join him there. She considered the proposed change totally unacceptable: "There was no way his plan was going to happen. The thought of going back to Jackson with all the bad memories and horrible things that had happened there, it was completely out of the question."[2] After careful consideration of her options and counseling, she concluded the best solution was to get a divorce and explore different career possibilities. She never returned to private practice.

News of her availability was quickly noticed. Offers came from across public and private sectors, including national federal agencies. Vigorous pursuers were quick to point out their reasons for being convinced she was their candidate of choice. They emphasized how much her training and work history was compatible with their mission, and expressed the extent to which their organization needed her. From the list of offers, she accepted the position as Team Physician at the North Lawndale Neighborhood Health Center (currently the Martin Luther King, Jr. Neighborhood Health Center) with The University of Chicago Medical School and Mount Sinai Hospital Department of Pediatrics.

The west side facility provided services that were on the cusp of new interventions in public health coming out of Washington, DC. The programs operated nationwide, and were at that time called the 330 and 660 Projects under the Health Resources and Services Administration (HRSA). Federally funded programs sprang up gradually across the country as intervention efforts in high mortality, mostly minority and hard-to-reach populations. Even though the daily drive to and from the new work location did not considerably improve, she had returned to the preferred medical service arena. The Lawndale Center position was salaried with convenient hours, including free weekends and evenings, and sufficient time to engage in other community interests.

During her second year at the center, Dr. Forbes was notified by a former colleague at Cook County Hospital that the distinguished medical scientist, Dr. Albert Dorfman, wanted to speak with her. The request alone impressed her because of his reputation. Dr. Dorfman (1916–1982) was a world-renowned researcher in biochemical genetics and birth defects. As the Richard T. Crane Memorial Professor and Chair of the Department of Pediatrics at the University of Chicago, he significantly influenced clinical medicine, genetics and developmental biology at the institution. Dr. Forbes was flattered that he wondered "if she would be willing to give him a call."

Formalities aside, it was apparent at the onset of their conversation that Dr. Dorfman was on a recruiting mission for the university and wanted to explore the possibility of bringing her on board. With her expressed willingness to proceed, he arranged for an interview. During the process, she was informed of the university's participation in national programs targeting high-risk populations in major cities that involved largely African-American neighborhoods, but also served Native American and Alaska native communities. In efforts to achieve maximum effectiveness, there was a national push to secure professionals who would likely be compatible with members of those demographics to participate in the programs. Plus, there was an immediate need for a pediatrician.

Dr. Dorfman initially became aware of Dr. Forbes' reputation from reading the *Chicago Tribune* article published a few years prior and took it from there. When the university developed a pressing need for someone with her experience and professional background, interest in her career resurfaced, and the possibility of her assisting the institution in achieving its goals was explored. Dr. Forbes, considered an excellent fit, was offered the position of assistant medical director at the Woodlawn Child Health Center (M&I Project) with a concurrent appointment teaching pediatrics at the medical school. She accepted on the spot.

The center's location on 63rd Street in what she described as "the back door of the University of Chicago" was closer to her South Side area residence than the site of the previous facility. Moreover, Woodlawn's reputation as a healthcare facility was enhanced by the fact that it operated out of the prestigious Pritzker School of Medicine Department of Pediatrics at the University. Dr. Forbes' arrival triggered a buzz of its own.

The new position made her the first African American woman to join the medical faculty at the University of Chicago, and only the second from the Black community overall. She joined Dr. James Edward Bowman, Jr. (1923–2011), who was hired in 1962. An expert in the fields of pathology and genetics, and an advocate for bioethics, Dr. Bowman began as an assistant professor and director of the hospital's blood bank. He was later promoted to tenured full professor, and mentored countless minority physician-scientists who went through the division's programs.

Dr. Forbes had her own contributions to make, joining the Department of Pediatrics that was composed of nearly forty faculty members with subspecialties in every imaginable category. It was a striking difference from what she was accustomed to from the past, where departments consisted of about eight or nine people, one of whom was responsible for supervising everything. Her transition was smooth. She adapted quickly and well to the university's academic environment, and her effectiveness was noted in the classroom and on 63rd Street.

The center was attractive and well-staffed, funded by Title 5 out of Washington, DC.[3] Patients were picked up and bused to their appointments. Woodlawn was essentially the only place where serious attempts were made by the establishment to interface with the local community. Evening neighborhood meetings were held there after the clinic closed, and it was the site of local weekend gatherings. The staff made concerted efforts for the health center to be accessible to young mothers affected by the turmoil in the city's streets, many of whom were girlfriends or otherwise associated with gang members or young men being sought by gangs. Sixty-Third Street was situated in the heart of the gang turf rivalry that existed primarily between the Blackstone Rangers and the Devil's Disciples.[4] The role of the clinic was duly noted by both.

The Woodlawn area became even more unstable following the assassination of Dr. Martin Luther King, Jr., in Memphis, Tennessee, on April 4, 1968. Among the more than one hundred cities across the US experiencing unrest, Chicago was the site of some of the worst riots, and the Woodlawn neighborhood experienced the majority of the city's destruction and chaos.[5] After thirty-six fires were reported between 4:00 pm and 10:00 pm on April 5, Mayor Richard J. Daley imposed a curfew and closed streets. More than 6,700 Illinois National Guard troops were brought in to support local police who were issued specific orders from the mayor to "shoot to kill any arsonist or anyone with a Molotov cocktail in his hand...and, to shoot to maim or cripple anyone looting any stores in our city."[6]

It was the first time Dr. Forbes practiced medicine under such challenging, socially charged circumstances. It clarified for her at least some of the reasons why she had appealed so much to the institution as a faculty member and as someone in leadership at the Center. The racial and cultural implications were undeniable.

> The Center was the mechanism for outreach from the university. Of course, I understood the other side of it, too. It was also designed so that minority patients did not clog up the hospital emergency room. My awareness of this type process went back to when I was at Cook County Hospital, where paddy wagons carrying injured Black patients passed Michael Reese and Mercy and were always brought to County Hospital. Federal programs were put strategically in place to be accessible to that patient population, but also to keep them out of the other hospital emergency rooms.[7]

Regardless of the university's ulterior motive, and despite the states of anxiety and concern that emerged in the face of social instability, under her leadership, the center staff held their ground and remained operational. After two days of rioting, the civil disturbance left eleven people dead, forty-eight others with gunshot wounds from police, ninety police officers injured and 2,150 citizens arrested. Dr. Forbes felt justified in taking the actions implemented, pointing out:

> There was a tremendous amount of fear that we were going to be either burned out, torn down, or affected negatively in any number of other ways by the riots. After the National Guard was called out and they continually patrolled Sixty-Third Street, the tension grew greatly. I was not afraid after all the things that happened—the burning and destruction of property all around us. But we were not touched. The only place that remained open and untouched in the area was the Woodlawn Child Health Center. People that I knew were concerned. They called and asked me, 'Are you going to work?' I told them, 'Of course, I'm going to work. It never really occurred to me not to go. You don't think about things like that when you work in medicine. We kept the center open. I continued seeing patients. I reminded everyone who called that many of the patients were small children and young women. They were a part of the community we served. We stayed in place and made ourselves available to them.[8]

The center remained unscathed.

Dr. Forbes persevered in the classroom as well, teaching pediatrics throughout the academic year in addition to being at the helm of service activities at the center. At the conclusion of the school year, she was presented with the opportunity to take a two-week leave. The professional time away from the university involved travel to four cities organized for a group of one hundred pediatricians. The Soviet-American Clinical Pediatric Conference included stops in Moscow and Leningrad (now St. Petersburg), Russia, Budapest, Hungary, and Vienna, Austria. She was one of three African Americans on the trip, the remaining two being a couple; and was paired with the only other single woman in the group, the widow of a recently deceased pediatrician.

The trip had a major impact on her because of the observed leadership of women in Moscow and Leningrad that far exceeded the impression made on her while she was in Africa. What struck her even more was that the situation seemed perfectly normal in the Russian environment, which was radically different from the norm in the US. She noted: "They were in charge of everything. Men were off in the military. This left women to serve as directors of hospitals, chairs of the departments and in charge of the surgery entities." The absence of men in the medical hierarchy in both cities was such a contrast to the male-predominated model in the US that it ignited a personal passion and mission in her that included hopes for her alma mater.[9]

> It said to me that women can do this; but also, it was as if I saw the future. I felt deeply that one day women were going to have a larger say in medicine in America. It was important for African American women to be ready to be a part of it. If they were going to participate, then Spelman had to lead the way because the college was the place where we were getting large numbers of Black women that were academically prepared. Many of them had been valedictorians and salutatorians of their high school graduating classes. That was my experience at Spelman.[10]

Lobbying for opportunities for Spelman women in fields of science was a priority for her the moment she joined the Spelman College Board of Trustees in 1966. Roots for the advocacy at the college dated back to her student days in the 1950s. As a faculty member and program affiliate at the University of Chicago, she participated in several alumnae events, serving as host for one fundraising reception for President Albert Manley held at the Faculty Club. Thirty fellow Spelman graduates attended. It turned out that Dr. John Hope Franklin, the John Matthews Manly Distinguished Service Professor in History at the University of Chicago, was Dr. Manley's best friend. President Manley routinely visited Dr. Franklin when he made business trips to the University of Chicago. Following the death of his wife, Dorothy Shepard Manley (1911–1964), President Manley was in a state of grief for approximately five years.[11] He made more frequent trips to Chicago as the house guest of Dr. Franklin. During those visits, Dr. Franklin often held dinners in his honor and Dr. Forbes, an accomplished Spelman alumna, was typically invited. Dr. Franklin and Dr. Forbes shared a guarded concern for President Manley, noticing his excessive weight loss and general state of unhappiness due to the loss of his wife.

Meanwhile, Dr. Forbes' academic and medical service experiences brought her to the attention of another large community-emphasized program. One day at work she received a phone call from a representative of the University of California in San Francisco. She was invited to San Francisco for an interview. Administrators were looking for a minority pediatrician to assist with the establishment of their C&Y project, the Children and Youth program funded by the federal government for the Fillmore and Haight-Ashbury communities. In addition to her professional reputation and specific expertise in pediatrics, she was considered to be an even more appealing candidate as someone already in the program. The university claimed concerted efforts had been made to secure assistance from minority professionals in the past, but they had been unsuccessful with attracting the help needed. They expressed hope the search would end with her.

The university made a strong case. As Dr. Forbes assessed the pros and cons carefully, she reflected on how she made a difference in the treatment of African American patients at Mercy Hospital in Gary, Indiana; tended to the needs of the South Side and West Side communities in Chicago at the Woodlawn Center during a critical period in the face of racial unrest; served patients and students well at Cook County Hospital and the University of Chicago in ways that improved opportunities for other African American women; and had effectively overseen and administered healthcare outreach to patients in Nigeria and Russia. Now, she had the chance to address health matters in another region of the country and experience life on the west coast at the same time. Although the position had its own set of requirements, it was anchored in a program with which she was fundamentally familiar.

Unaccustomed to what was going on specifically in the area where the program was housed or the State in general, she was open to a new challenge and engagement that promised to broaden the scope of her knowledge and medical experience. The idea of a cultural and physical change of scenery was appealing, especially the thought of having access to breathtaking west coastal views, iconic landmarks and legendary California Redwoods. She accepted the university's offer and became Assistant Director for Ambulatory Pediatrics and C&Y Project at Mount Zion Hospital and Medical Center.

Dr. Forbes noticed early on that, in at least one case, the situation in northern California was not radically different from that she observed on the South Side of Chicago. Like before, the only source of medical treatment for African Americans in the Fillmore District was at Mount Zion Hospital through the auspices of the University of California in San Francisco. This was operationally in much the same manner that Black residents on the South Side of Chicago were compelled to rely on the University of Chicago's relationship with the Woodlawn Clinic for healthcare.[12] On the other hand, Haight-Ashbury presented quite a different scenario.

The neighborhood was crumbling at the time of her arrival and while its large African American population was similarly dependent when it came to medical care, the community had become the nation's main hippie and counterculture district of the 1960s.[13] The prevalence of drug use, especially the methamphetamine speed, was immediately evident. It was a common occurrence for young women who were high on the drug to leave their three- or four-week-old babies unattended in empty apartments. Seeing young mothers who were completely out of it due to substance abuse was the most difficult situation Dr. Forbes witnessed up to that point. Fortunately, there was considerable pediatric mobilization around the communities that removed children from such homes and temporarily housed and cared for them until their mothers were either off drugs or in an improved situation to the advantage of their infants. It was an extremely busy program.

Dr. Forbes had not dealt with drug problems at the Chicago center but recognized the phenomenon would not remain a California concern—that substance abuse would spread rapidly from populous regions like the west coast into the heartland and other parts of America. She vigorously advocated for health system staffs to learn everything possible about the nature and implications of such drug abuse for the sake of establishing proactive treatment measures. She felt it was imperative for appropriate agencies to become prepared to address ramifications of substance abuse in terms of overall public health, especially, from her perspective, its negative impact on infants. Having to attend to the medical needs of newborns and young children of addicted parents was unforeseen, but broadened the scope of her professional experience, and underscored her consideration of increasing ways in which Spelman graduates could become involved in medical science in the future. Her thoughts along such lines about healthcare invariably turned to possibilities at Spelman.

Serving on the Board of Trustees at Spelman remained a priority. As such, she was able to lobby in favor of strengthening the science curriculum at the college. She elaborated,

> The time had come when we could no longer depend on Morehouse courses to provide the preparation necessary in science for Spelman women. One or two graduates a year in the field was not enough. We needed to increase not only the matriculation numbers but expand recruiting efforts as well. In order to get good science students, it was necessary to engage high schools and identify the female students with an affinity for and an interest in science. We needed to increase course offerings and enlarge the faculty. As a Trustee, I had a stronger voice regarding things that I thought were going to happen in science and medicine, especially for Black Americans. It turned out I was right.[14]

The relationship between Dr. Forbes and President Manley changed after she relocated to San Francisco and attended the Spelman Board of Trustees meeting in New York in 1969. Their previous interaction at board meetings and during the president's fundraising trips to Chicago had been platonic, Spelman goal-centered, and occurred in group settings with limited one-on-one engagement. In fact, Dr. Forbes had been such a career-oriented and focused advocate for women in the profession by example, through opportune conversations with healthcare leaders and during college board meetings, that the few social engagements which did occur were related to those efforts.

Prior concern about President Manley's emotional state of grieving which threatened his physical well-being—an observation she shared with Dr. Franklin—waned as he persevered with fundraising events for Spelman. Dr. Forbes had become one of the most consistent and most generous alumna givers who supported institutional advancement events in Chicago. A mutual fondness developed between them. She considered him a caring person who was deeply committed to the college. The new phase in her personal life placed her in a commuting situation once again. The relationship progressed when he subsequently invited her to Jamaica over a Christmas holiday break and she accepted.

When the president proposed, Dr. Forbes was caught off-guard, not having considered their relationship had advanced to such a degree. Initially, she was hesitant to respond, but after considerable thought, she eventually told herself: *Think for a minute. Why wouldn't you marry him?* She accepted his proposal and agreed to move to Atlanta on the condition that she would continue her medical career. She explained,

> I had no vision of myself being married to a professional man like the president of Spelman College, becoming first lady and having to plan and host teas or whatever events needed to be arranged, and not continuing my career. Fortunately, he had no problem with my wishes. In fact, he believed there were plenty of opportunities available to me in Atlanta. He went further by firmly indicating he would be happy for me to continue my career.[15]

It was obvious to her that they were on the same page.

In early fall, less than two months before the start of the academic year, Dr. Audrey Forbes and Dr. Albert Manley were married in San Francisco. They proceeded to visit Mrs. Sally Sage McAlpin (1931–1992), chair of the Spelman College Board of Trustees, in time for the fall meeting in New York. Audrey

Manley and Mrs. McAlpin had worked well together over the four years since she joined the college's board, with the chair being consistently supportive of her requests and recommendations. The couple's plan to travel to Jamaica on their honeymoon immediately following the conclusion of the August meeting was interrupted when President Manley received an urgent call from Atlanta informing him that a four-alarm fire had totally destroyed Morgan Hall. The one piece of good news was that the lone occupant in the building had escaped without injury.

Morgan Hall was dedicated in 1901 as a dining and residence hall named for General Thomas Jefferson Morgan, corresponding secretary of American Baptist Home Missionary Society (ABHMS).[16] In addition to meeting student needs, Morgan Hall once was the site of high-profile community and social events such as a Testimonial Banquet honoring Mrs. Lugenia Burns Hope on July 11, 1933, attended by more than one hundred nationally prominent African Americans.[17] News of the building's destruction led the couple to hurry back to Atlanta.

President Manley made his way quickly to campus to deal with the implications of the property loss along with the scope of usual college leadership responsibilities. Dr. Audrey Manley returned to her alma mater, intending to build on the wealth of knowledge and firsthand experiences in medical science already realized in ways that would benefit Spelman and her career. Her sights continued to remain on advocating for increased opportunities for African American women in healthcare with Spelman playing a pivotal role. It was 1970.

CHAPTER 8

First Lady at Spelman

Arriving on campus as the first alumna first lady of the college, Dr. Audrey Manley gave serious consideration to how she might best serve Spelman and, at the same time, meet her personal and professional needs as a physician. Her record as a practitioner, administrator, and advocate of advances for women in healthcare careers primed her for pursuing measures to position Spelman in the forefront of training women for leadership in medical science.

Loyalty to her career was matched by a commitment to her husband, the college, and their home. She devoted the first six months on campus to updating Reynolds Cottage, the Victorian-style official residence of the president built in 1901. Assisted by employees in Buildings and Grounds, the living areas underwent renovation while the attic and basement were cleared out and reorganized for more efficient storage use. Shortly after the desired make-over of Reynolds Cottage was complete, as she contemplated the best approach to take to attend to career matters, three Spelman students showed up unexpectedly at the Reynolds Cottage door. They made it clear in no time that the unscheduled visit was to solicit her help.

Virginia Davis Floyd, Denise Barefield-Pendleton, and Pamela Gunter-Smith came to speak with her regarding Tapley Hall. They wondered if she had been in the building since returning to Spelman. Indicating she had not, they stated simply: "We will not say anything further, but you need to go and see it."[1] They left it at that. In no time, Tapley was the target of her discreet investigation. A detailed tour of the building made the basis of the students' concerns obvious. Dr. Manley noticed right away that Tapley's condition was far from ideal. One reason for the building's poor physical state had to do with the work of Dr. Barnett F. Smith. Dr. Smith was Chairman of the Department of Biology specializing in parasitology—the study of parasites, organisms that live on or in a host and get its food from or at the expense of its host, and can cause disease in humans. To facilitate his research, Dr. Smith kept live chickens on the premises in a closet located very near the entrance to Tapley Hall. It was a touchy situation that needed immediate attention, but Dr. Audrey Manley knew any action taken needed to come directly from the president.

She decided to take a subtle approach. After serving the president his usual evening martini and having dinner, she posed the same question to him that had been put to her, inquiring if he had been inside Tapley Hall recently. His "no" answer prompted her to suggest that he do so. Adhering to her request, President Manley walked through the building to view its condition for himself. He recognized the need to do something immediately about it, and took measures to rectify the situation. Once the livestock issue was corrected, Dr. Audrey Manley knew she had the president's ear regarding making additional improvements at Tapley Hall and in regards to additional science-related matters. Although she was concerned about a number of other issues, and was more than willing to share ideas with the president about them, her primary goal at that juncture was to attend to career options.

Dr. Audrey Manley made an appointment with the chairman of the Pediatrics Department at the Emory University School of Medicine, Dr. Richard Winston Blumberg (1914–2000), to explore what opportunities might be available to her. Their interaction went well. Dr. Blumberg informed her that a primary concern at that time was teenage pregnancy, a nationwide problem being addressed at Emory through a unified effort of the Department of Pediatrics and the Department of Obstetrics and Gynecology (OB/GYN). In the hope that she would help, he introduced her to the chair of the Department of Obstetrics and Gynecology, Dr. John Daniel Thompson, Sr. (1927–2017). Dr. Blumberg further explained that the two units had established a program together to address teenage pregnancy at Grady Memorial Hospital. It was a unique model program, being the only instance in the country where Pediatrics and OB/GYN departments came together to deal with teen pregnancy.

Their dialogue led to an offer and Dr. Manley's acceptance of a joint faculty position in the Department of Pediatrics and the Department of Obstetrics and Gynecology. This marked the first time for such an unprecedented dual appointment, and simultaneously made Dr. Audrey Forbes Manley the first African American woman to serve on the faculty of the medical school. In addition to teaching, she assisted Dr. Robert Anthony Hatcher (b. 1937), Director of the Emory University Family Planning Program at Grady Hospital, and had oversight of Emory residents at the hospital.

Teenage pregnancy had not been an area of particular emphasis during her training or work experience in the past, but she realized its connectivity to pediatric matters, and took measures to expand her knowledge of the subject in order to assure her effective support of program efforts. Dr. Manley enrolled in an eight-week program on the topic conducted out of the Region IV (Atlanta) Office of the US Department of Health and Human Services (HHS).

When she was better informed, one of her first plans was to initiate a teenage Emory University/Grady Memorial Hospital Family Planning Clinic. Dr. Manley served as Chief of Medical Services (1972–1976), oversaw the establishment of the sexually-transmitted diseases (STDs) and Family Planning clinic for pediatric patients, and assisted with the formation of two evening clinic services operated under the Obstetrics and Gynecology Department. She was very happy with what had been accomplished through joint efforts of Pediatrics and OB/GYN at Grady Hospital, but was not completely happy because no final arrangements for funds had been made.

She was concerned that no funds were channeled to benefit HBCUs on the southside of Atlanta. Dr. Manley contended that the young people on the southside of the city had equal needs to those of the young women at the Grady Hospital Clinic in terms of health education and service relative to sexual activity. She noted,

> I saw it so clearly. When students attending schools on the southside completed their study, they typically went back to their home environments and assumed leadership roles in their communities. These young women and men, as future leaders, needed to be sufficiently equipped with viable information about reproduction and contraception.[2]

Dr. Manley stated her case about the practicality of more equitable opportunities on the southside to Emory officials. She was firm, methodical, and blunt. The desired result came in relatively short order. She indicated, "it was not a major battle. I won that one pretty easily, but had to learn when the meeting was held, otherwise, I would have missed the opportunity to speak to them."[3] Moving forward, she knew Andrea Jackson, Region IV Health Administrator for the HHS, could solve this problem. Dr. Manley went to her for help and advice.

A $25,000 subcontract from the Emory University federal grant allowed her to initiate family planning services at Spelman College that benefited the entire Atlanta University Center. Additional support for the Family Planning program came from a Title X Service Grant in cooperation with Emory University.

Dr. Manley's pre-knowledge of the need for Family Planning initiatives in the southern region of the country dated back to when she was chief resident at Cook County Hospital in Chicago. Upon her return to Georgia, it was a public health matter that she was strongly, and continually, urged to address by health professionals from across the country. She also secured contributions from The Charles Edward Merrill Trust.

The Family Planning Program and Initiative began operations in 1972 in McVicar Hospital. The out-patient clinic provided routine care of students along with gynecology and contraceptive counseling, as well as information and services on Mondays through Thursdays from 5 pm until 8 pm.[4] The additional resources made it possible to hire health educator Doris McLittle and nurse practitioner, Judith Gordon Tate. Dr. Elijah Jones was the medical physician in charge.

McLittle was trained in clinical psychology (BA) and public health (MPH) with a concentration in population and family planning from the University of Michigan. She contended that the program emphasized family planning as a concept and a health entity for planning your future life. McLittle taught elective courses related to the topic, including Family Planning and Population Growth.

Judith Gordon (Tate), studied nursing at the University of Colorado, earned a master's degree in adult psychiatric nursing from Wayne State University and was completing additional study at Emory University. She expressed hope that the program would have a long-range impact on students as they enter their professional, social, and private lives.[5]

Amid reservations about family planning as a clinical program in its own right, and as a component to the provision of healthcare to students at the Women's Health Clinic, Dr. Audrey Manley, program medical personnel, and other staff members articulated its core mission and numerous physical and mental benefits of the program. Doris McLittle extended the education component to include special sessions, dorm visits, and informal meetings with student groups. Judith Gordon (Tate) incorporated the dissemination of information with the administration of care during student visits.

One consistent voice of support outside of the clinic came from Reverend (Dr.) Norman M. Rates. Rev. Rates served as college minister, Professor of Religion, and Chair of the Department of Philosophy and Religion for over forty-eight years beginning in 1954. He was an influential figure at the college during the Civil Rights Movement in addition to his role as a respected faculty member college-wide. Rev. Rates was attributed with having "established the spiritual foundation of the campus and ensured a sound moral and ethical community for generations of Spelman women."[6] He applauded Dr. Manley's commitment, determination, and tact in supporting the program.[7] Rev. Rates expressed his appreciation for the manner in which she took family planning, sex education, and related issues "out of the gutter of our minds and put it up front and center for discussion" in the interest of physical and emotional health.[8]

Eventually, Dr. Manley successfully implemented a more effective operational model for the Women's Health Clinic. A nurse practitioner manned the campus facility on a daily basis, with referral support from external physicians when necessary.[9] Judith Gordon, the nurse practitioner, became the service director. As the medical school professional with oversight of interns and residents at Emory University, Dr. Audrey Manley assigned two African American resident physicians in OB/GYN from Grady Hospital to provide medical services at MacVicar on Tuesdays and Thursdays from 5 until 8 pm. Dr. Mack Arthur Jones (1942–2004) and Dr. Samuel Lightfoot, Sr. (1941–2004) were among the first to assist.

The Women's Health Clinic provided an educational opportunity for Spelman students. The first students to take advantage of this opportunity were Mamie Earnestine Phillips, junior pre-med, and Lillian Ashe, sophomore pre-med. They were taught to take histories; weigh patients; check blood pressure; and assist in administering routine exams, tests, and other procedures; and monitor a range of medical conditions—all the things they could do in a doctor's office. Andrea Jackson, in her capacity with the Atlanta Regional Office of the United States Public Health Service (USPHS), was supportive of the program that was developed.

By the fall of 1974, the clinic had gone from having two physicians on site twice a week to offering service Monday through Friday, with two full-time doctors on staff. The general healthcare program was headed by Dr. Clinton E. Warner assisted by Dr. Elisha Jones, and nurse clinicians Virginia Smith and Cathrow Hardaway. An advisory committee was established, including members from each of the AUC Schools: Mrs. Jean Chandler, Clark College; Mrs. Althea Truitt, Atlanta University; Dr. Elynor P. Brown, Morehouse College; Mrs. Elmyra Rumph, Morris Brown College; and Dr. Audrey Manley, Spelman College.

Dr. Manley was instrumental to the formation of the Georgia R. Dwelle Health Careers Office in 1971, which was named in honor of the first graduate of Spelman to attend medical school, Dr. Georgia Rooks Dwelle (1884–1977)—a native of Atlanta in the class of 1900The Spelman College Health Careers Program was established with a primary goal to increase the number of highly qualified minority women entering the health and allied health professions, along with the commitment to eradicate health illiteracy by providing a strong educational foundation for Spelman students to educate the communities they moved on to serve.

Support for the Health Careers Office came from two sources. A $25,000 grant was received from The Association of American Medical Colleges (AAMC), a nonprofit organization in Washington, DC. Another $25,000 grant came from The Josiah Macy Jr. Foundation (Macy Foundation), a philanthropic foundation in New York. Both organizations had national programs committed to increasing the number of Black physicians in America. The Macy Foundation had a national program dedicated to "improving health by advancing the education and training of health professionals."[10] The AAMC was committed to providing programs for students and faculty to encourage their interest in healthcare careers.

Dr. Audrey Manley's office located in the Old Laundry Building on Spelman's campus served as the Health Careers Office. Shelves were installed along the walls to display admissions catalogs for every medical school in the country. Practice sessions for taking the MCAT were held for students attending any of the Atlanta University Center institutions. There were summer experiences for students in federal, state, local, and private settings to give them practical experience on what the health community, health fields, and medical practice were about. African American doctors were solicited to open their medical offices on Saturdays so that Spelman students could shadow them and observe the nature of providing private practice care first hand.[11]

Dr. Manley attended to patients and administered oversight of Emory University residents and interns at Grady Memorial Hospital during the day. One or two hours after work each evening and on Saturdays, she volunteered at the Health Careers Office in addition to chairing the Health Careers Advisory Committee.

Curriculum development in science at Spelman occurred during the same period of time, which led to the establishment of the Division of Natural Sciences in 1972 under President Albert Manley. The president named Mathematics Professor Dr. Shirley Mathis McBay (1935–2021) as chair. When President Manley later announced his retirement plans effective June 30, 1976, Dr. Audrey Manley began thinking about her next career move. She had a good experience at Emory but decided to look around, put out feelers, and remain open to the next adventure. Her more recent experience in family planning, family planning training, teaching at Emory, running the cooperative program at Grady Hospital, and things she started at Spelman strengthened her already highly regarded work history.

She received several offers. The initial opportunities came from the National Heart Institute, National Lung Institute, and the HRSA. HRSA was most appealing, being the home of all the programs she had worked with around the country over previous years. The projects at the University of Chicago came out of HRSA, as well as the work she did in California and at Emory.

She, admittedly, did not see the big picture even after completing those work assignments until she was interviewed at HRSA. During an interview, she suddenly made the connection, commenting, "Oh, this is where the money has been coming from…this is the national office." It was underscored that maternal and child health; family planning; teenage pregnancy; heart, lung, and blood disease services were all funded out of HRSA in Washington, DC.

Dr. Manley was summoned to Washington one Friday to attend three scheduled interviews. The final interview was conducted by Assistant Surgeon General Dr. Edward Dana Martin, director of the Bureau for Health Care Delivery. The agency administered programs that provided resources for medical care throughout the nation. It included programs Dr. Manley had worked in and a number of additional programs she was aware of, all without completely understanding at the time of her employment exactly where the funding came from or the bases for its receipt prior to the interviews.

"Specific information about funding was essentially never in my purview," she explained. "It was the delivery of services and that is what I remained focused on. However, within minutes after I walked into Dr. Martin's office, as we talked and I learned of the breadth of the programs housed in the agency, I realized that was the place for me." Despite this awareness, she did not commit right away, remembering that her final decision had personal life and professional implications. In addition to the future of her career, President Manley's well-being had to be considered.

She returned to Atlanta the following Monday morning, went directly to the clinic, and was seeing patients when she received a call from HRSA. It was Dr. Martin, inquiring, "When can we expect you?" She replied, "Dr. Martin, I have not even made up my mind yet. I just saw you Friday. When do you need me?" He stressed, "We needed you yesterday." His reply was unexpected. However, she felt a general sense of compatibility with the agency and was committed to public health service. She admitted: "It was an appealing gesture on Dr. Martin's part, even though I did not grasp at that moment exactly what he meant by needing me yesterday." The basis for Dr. Martin's eagerness for her arrival notwithstanding, Dr. Manley accepted on the condition that she give

Emory University at least a thirty-day notice. She insisted on not leaving earlier than that. The mandated notification timeline to the university was honored, and her acceptance of the HRSA position was confirmed.

Her thirty-day notice to Emory coincided with the prearranged thirty-day vacation month with the institution. Instead of spending the time on rest and relaxation, Dr. Manley devoted it to preparing for the transition. Finding a house was a first priority along with the delicate task of convincing her husband that they had to move to Washington, DC. She fully grasped how tactful she needed to be: "He was a Southern man to say the least, having lived comfortably in North Carolina and Georgia. He envisioned us settling down in Atlanta after his retirement. Once President Manley realized that I was offered an outstanding job in Washington, DC, he agreed to relocate."[12]

While Spelman moved forward with plans to install Dr. Donald Mitchell Stewart (1938–2019) as the sixth president of the college, Dr. Albert Manley and Dr. Audrey Forbes Manley moved from Atlanta to the nation's capital. Arriving in Washington, DC, Dr. Albert Manley was hopeful of a smooth transition to retirement; Dr. Audrey Manley was optimistic about the next chapter in her healthcare career. It was August 1976.

CHAPTER 9

A New Beginning in Washington, DC

Relocation to Washington, DC, was facilitated by Dr. Audrey Manley making an advance trip to the city to find them a home and orchestrate transference of their combined accumulation of books, furniture, and other belongings. Soon afterward, they moved in and she went to work. Her thoughts turned often to Albert, wanting to make sure he acclimated well to the new situation, found his niche, and was happy. She knew the changes brought on from retiring were not easy for him, but hoped he would adapt within a reasonable amount of time. She witnessed his daily struggle, which caused emotional discomfort for her as well.

> It did not happen right away. Two-and-a-half years passed before he settled into being in Washington and adjusted to not being at the top of the society list. Howard University president, Dr. James Edward Cheek [1932–2010], was very kind to him.[1] Dr. Cheek was a good friend. He gave Albert an office on the law school campus. There were several Spelman and Morehouse graduates attending the law school at Howard who constantly ran in and out of his office. He finally began to become comfortable, but it was not easy.[2]

Dr. Audrey Manley joined the ranks of the HRSA expecting the national leadership to address the need to improve the quality of healthcare available to minority patients and that the agency would probably play a central role.

> I had no vision of how it would happen; but I knew what the situation was in Jackson, Mississippi; what I saw in Chicago; and then, what I witnessed in Russia and Africa. America was behind. We had very sophisticated facilities such as the University of Chicago and Emory University, but we were not keeping up in terms of putting front line doctors out there to treat these lesser-served patients. I suppose I never really fully understood how the funding worked. I was too busy

> taking care of patients. But at Health Resources and Services Administration (HRSA), I understood the capacity for funding to not only provide high-powered medical technology but to also provide optimum care of patients everywhere.[3]

One matter that had gained considerable attention at the time of her arrival at the agency was SC disease, a cause that was taken on to a certain extent during the Richard M. Nixon administration. SC disease was barely on the national medical radar prior to the late 1960s. The disease was medically described as early as 1910, but drew little public attention and virtually no funding support for several decades. Although there was a rapid screening test based on a simple finger stick, it was seldom used until the emergence of local clinics around 1970.

In 1965, two physician-activists—H. Jack Geiger and Count D. Gibson, Jr.—opened the first community health centers in Boston, Massachusetts, and Mount Bayou, Mississippi, to heighten awareness of the omission of SC disease from the attention of medical entities. Geiger and Gibson believed that quality health could not be fully achieved without addressing poverty. The Black Panther Party took the argument further, articulating that the failure to address poverty along with oppression, unemployment, lack of adequate education, and housing were interconnected root causes of poor health. Emphasizing their recognition of sickle cell anemia as a neglected genetic disease because the majority of those affected were Blacks, the Black Panther Party launched many of the earliest SC disease campaigns in the nation and initiated programs highlighted with the opening of free health clinics in various locations across the country.

The National Sickle Cell Anemia Control Act, signed by President Richard M. Nixon on May 16, 1972, appeared to change the medical landscape for citizens suffering from the illness and improve levels of research among medical scientists working to treat and combat the disease. Ten million dollars was allocated that year, increasing to $16 million in 1973 in accordance with the bill's enactment, which, along with funds to provide healthcare services to sickle cell patients, brought broader attention to the disease. However, addressing this particular medical problem triggered an unanticipated response.

There were ten sickle cell research centers funded by NIH established at some of the nation's leading hospitals such as the ones at Boston University, the University of Chicago, and the University of California, San Francisco. People with a general interest in SC anemia, persons who wanted to learn more about the disease for any number of reasons, and those individuals who recognized the inefficiency and lack of services to SC patients organized and beat on the doors of the bureau. Dr. Manley referred to them as "meet you at the pavement" kind of grassroots individuals who insisted that something be done expeditiously about sickle cell disease. Their lobbying efforts perpetuated the passage of legislation covering sickle cell disease, which occurred under President Nixon.

When it was time to renew the legislation in 1976, advocates of funding for other hereditary diseases decided to launch lobby campaigns of their own. This resulted in the new legislation providing for the treatment of nine diseases, Tay–Sachs, cystic fibrosis, etc., along with sickle cell anemia. At that point, other genetic disease operations began to compete with the sickle cell programs for available funds. Once aware of the background—the related courses of events leading up to the time she was hired by the bureau—Dr. Manley began to understand what she had gotten into. She had envisioned a much less complicated routine of "going into a nice office, sitting behind a nice desk and writing letters or whatever on Washington stationery, not being caught in the middle of a battle for funds. I knew about sickle cell disease and I knew about the other diseases. What I did not know about was the legislation and what the new bill did. It pitted the various genetic disease entities against each other for the dollars that were now available." Things were literally brewing while she waited to board her flight at the departure gate at Hartsfield International Airport in Atlanta, was in the air, and landed in Washington, DC. The moment she physically showed up at the office, she stepped into a major fight.

> I had to absorb things overnight realizing that I had walked into a hornet's nest. It was clear why Dr. Martin needed me 'yesterday.' He needed a Black doctor because it was not likely that the sickle cell people would have trusted anybody to deal with them fairly in the forward movement of genetic diseases unless the person was African American. There was the possibility that I may not have been considered a good fit, not exactly being someone who was street-wise and having moved from one academic community to another. But I had gone through the Cook County experience. That was something.[4]

She determined further:

> There was no way in the world I was going to shut them down. I would have been afraid for anybody to go to Washington and try to shut down the sickle cell clinics. I believe the person who brought me in knew that. I was partly hired to deal

> with the sickle cell verbiage, outrage, and protests as this genetic disease policy was being implemented to make sure they were heard and did not get left out.[5]

Delivery of healthcare in America was beginning to change. Dr. Manley had been a part of it when working with Dr. Joseph Greengard in Illinois. Dr. Greengard insisted that the University of Chicago, Michael Reese, and Mount Sinai Hospitals in Chicago administer care to their share of the minority patients that were previously all shipped across town to Cook County.

At HRSA, she was thrust into an awareness of what serious funding battles were. In her assessment, these were "not boxing gloves, but bare knuckles fights." The implications of availability of financial resources were intensely felt, and players facilitating and implementing programs and policy were various. Fierce competition erupted between units desiring federal support on the one hand, while on the other, intragovernmental tugs of war for access and control existed from agencies such as the National Institute of Health, which wanted—and thought they should have—the resources to channel into research. HRSA did not agree and determined that the funds would remain with the agency for the delivery of care and service.

Initially, three million dollars was earmarked for sickle cell disease that was likely dispersed throughout the known twenty clinics across the country. The following legislation started off with sixteen million dollars including the three million for sickle cell disease. As the sickle cell people requested their money, other genetic disease entities expected funds, wanting to know how much HRSA was going to distribute to them and insisting they should receive their share. By then, two thousand genetic diseases had been identified and the number was growing. According to NIH, they were unlocking genetic codes for illnesses faster than agencies could keep up, despite technology being unveiled for the treatment of various diseases at a rapid rate.

Dr. Manley had to maintain the treacherous balance of taking necessary measures to harness research, and the service and education of those involved with genetic diseases in such a way that sickle cell disease funding was not compromised. Fear that the new round of money would go to NIH for research or for treatment of such diseases as cystic fibrosis with sickle cell programs getting nothing was fuel for action. Activists of sickle cell entities knew their cause had led the way, since the first legislation designated three million dollars for the disease. They made trips to Washington regularly, banged on doors demanding the release of funds promised, and inquired about what her office was specifically going to do before she was fully orientated in the position. They made the most noise, demonstrating in the halls of federal buildings until her boss said, "Where is she (meaning Dr. Manley)? Get her out here." Keeping peace was a tough job, but she was the person expected to do it.

While "thankful to the Lord every day for the invaluable experiences afforded her," she was challenged by the fact that the bill's provision was not a lot of money, even though she optimistically believed it could grow. Further, with such a large number of genetic diseases identified, her job was to honestly assess the bottom-line implications of what they had, what could be done, and what was needed, while also projecting for the future.

She navigated through the process successfully with a considerable amount of outside help. The March of Dimes was the first to offer support. As the primary organization in terms of history and credibility on the genetic disease front, the March of Dimes shared priceless information with her, advised her on tactical approaches in preparation for problems that inevitably lie ahead, and offered insight into how serious the situation could become if not handled properly. Additional organizations and knowledgeable individuals gradually came forward to assist her. She established relationships with more groups, listened to them, and acted on their advice. She recorded meetings that were transcribed into workable documents.

Dr. Manley was familiar with the workings of universities, especially the research side of things, and developed the ability to relate to people who took the initiative to run community based genetic organizations because no one else was doing it. She formed advisory committees made up of faculty from universities across the nation—Boston University, University of Virginia, University of California at San Francisco, University of Chicago, etc., noting the three focal areas were blood, cells, and biochemistry that spawned genetic diseases.

There were people of great stature conducting research in their labs with no mechanism for getting their results out. People were providing care for young sufferers of genetic diseases by working on their own in living rooms and dining rooms trying to help each other. Young researchers were exploring chromosome illnesses that no one understood at the time except a handful of faculty members.

She brought together the largest advisory committee ever, with the community and academic sides covered, as were representatives of entities connected to all nine diseases listed in the legislation, plus whatever the program perspective deemed most needed. The scientists and groups of advisors made sure everything that should be covered was covered, and everything that could wait was put on the back burner. The main questions for her became: How do we get that information out? How do we instruct people who need education in the three areas? How do we dispense the money in such a way that we get effective results?

Her next major undertaking was bringing the various competing entities together for the sake of moving forward. Dr. Manley determined progress was also dependent on ending the fighting. They would not be able to get money needed from Congress if the battles continued. Bringing grassroots people and chairmen of departments of cytogenetics, biochemistry, and hematology at universities across the country together was mutually beneficial and improved chances of getting more needed money from Congress. Being a good steward of allocated funds and making the most resourceful plan for the future was her approach. She implemented PL (Public Law)-92-463 related to the public diseases. It could have been interpreted either way, namely, the legislation could be limited to the named diseases or it could be expanded to include all genetic diseases. Ultimately, she successfully implemented the Genetic Diseases Act, aided in part with a review process.

The hardest task was going to every sickle cell clinic in operation to make sure they met federal standards. Those doing creditable work that the bureau could justify continued to receive financial resources. Those that did not were defunded. Grassroots programs connected to universities with oversight of a senior professor were more likely to be successful and survive than independent clinics run by nonprofessionals with little understanding of the ramifications of their efforts beyond doing testing. An exemplary operative was the Virginia Sickle Cell Disease Center initiated at the Medical Center of Virginia (MCV) in 1972 with a community center coordinator and pioneer SC disease awareness and research advocate Florence Neal Cooper Smith, and university hematologist Dr. Robert E. Scott at the helm. It represented the type of cooperation HRSA looked for.

There were a number of community clinics that had to be phased out due to noncompliance with criteria for continuance. Their elimination caused political backlash. On one occasion Dr. Manley was called to the director's office to explain the compliance process. Congressmen from Southern California wanted to know why clinics in their districts had lost funding. She was convinced that they expected someone "young and inexperienced who did not know what they were doing, hoping they could apply enough pressure to result in restoration of the money they were there to protect." Instead, she showed up and told them in no uncertain terms how the established guidelines formed the basis for assessments, what was being done at the clinics in question, and why they lost funding. Her concluding statement was: "If you would like to change it, be my guest," referring to the standards mandated by the federal government.

The bureau was fast learning not only about SC disease but other blood disorders like thalassemia, an inherited blood disorder that causes the body to have less hemoglobin than normal, hemoglobin enabling red blood cells to carry oxygen. They were also becoming more informed about chromosome diseases like trisomy, which may cause intellectual disorders, one of the medical conditions Dr. Manley had observed in patients when she was a Resident.[6]

> Most emphatic was how the count for genetic diseases had swelled from the one that we knew about in 1976, hypothyroidism, to two thousand. Knowledge of the prevalence of genetic diseases had caused monetary support to soar. Not only had Congressional funding continued, many grassroots and local efforts were receiving their own funding. Sickle cell disease among African Americans, cystic fibrosis within the White population, and chromosome problems since NIH rapidly turned over chromosome counts and identifying those conditions that really are the result of either abnormal numbers or makeup of the chromosomes, were the largest recipients of support.[7]

By this time, physicians were into amniocentesis and prenatal diagnoses. It was decided by the office that major funding would go into newborn screening, which would facilitate identification of the diseases early enough to make intervention possible. In prenatal cases, if treatment was available, mothers could be treated at that point. If treatment was not possible, parents had the difficult decision to make whether to continue the pregnancy or not. The field of genetics, especially in terms of the study of genetics in the newborn, grew rapidly during her tenure at HRSA. In this regard, they went from addressing hypothyroidism at her arrival in 1976, to screening thirty-seven diseases in the newborn when she left with the continued support of the March of Dimes.

The increase reflected a tremendous amount of work by her HRSA office and collaborators, considerable use of technology, and a lot of university laboratory input. Learning more about chromosome diseases; marking progress with the assistance of the March of Dimes, which had been working in the field in this area for fifteen years; and channeling information and support to local community entities perpetuated an interactive structural network.

Money was designated for newborn technologies. With the genetic disease program no longer requiring daily attention by her office, and being safely housed in the Office of Maternal and Child Health, funding continued to flow to individual states and a few organizations like the March of Dimes that were doing approved research, education programs, and services. The research component was under NIH, and the Centers for Disease Control and Prevention (CDC) provided all laboratory oversight, including that of reputable grass-root sickle cell clinics. They were at a turning point and at the ten-year mark, Dr. Manley needed a break. She informed her boss of her decision to enroll at Johns Hopkins as a year-long Public Health Service (PHS) fellow to earn a master's of public health degree. She emphasized before leaving that upon her return, she wanted a different job. "I had finished what I was brought in to do with genetic diseases, and wanted to take some much-needed time off. The PHS traineeship was a treasure—a twenty-five thousand dollar scholarship for the year at Johns Hopkins, along with my salary."

It turned out to be far from the easy year in Baltimore she anticipated. Dr. Manley was much older than her classmates. No campus housing was available, prompting her to rent an efficiency apartment where a number of other Johns Hopkins students lived, and she had to commute every day. She was unable to get a garage space where she lived, and had to park outside, an inconvenience when snow removal was necessary in winter. The first Monday morning class was computer technology. Knowing nothing about computers, she wondered if her move was a big mistake. After getting some much-needed technology help, she suffered through it and came out okay thanks to the assistance of a classmate, Dr. Sherry Rodgers, MD. After every lecture, she had a follow-up tutoring session with Dr. Rodgers.

Study sessions in the library often lasted until three or four in the morning, much too late to go home, so everyone slept on tables, a difficult feat at her age, but she got through that, too.

She actually found living like a student again somewhat rewarding. Dr. Manley particularly enjoyed and benefited from being exposed to the foreign students. Her classmates included medical professionals from health departments all over the world that had ties to Johns Hopkins. Sponsored by their governments, they were sent to Hopkins to learn the latest healthcare developments. In addition to gaining insight from their various points of view, she made new friends in the field. Dr. Manley completed the program in the designated time and returned to Washington, DC, with the master's degree in public health in hand.

Amid career successes, personal tragedy struck again in 1987. It was worse than before. She recounted:

> Barbara is the only full sister I have. She had two children, Denise and Kimberly. I was very much involved with Barbara and the early rearing of her children. My relationship with Denise, the oldest, was as close to having a child as I would get. She was the first born of the two and she had my name, Denise Elaine. Of course, as far as I was concerned, they were both destined for Spelman. Kimberly attended Spelman then went on to Meharry Dental School before completing her degree at Tennessee State University. Denise was attending the University of South Florida working on a master's degree when she had a fatal automobile accident. Apparently, it had rained, the pavement was slick and the car skidded. She was a good girl. I don't know why the Lord took her so early. It was the worst pain in my life. It caused me more pain than the loss of my mother.[8]

Dr. Manley returned to work at the bureau as Director of the National Health Service Corps (NHSC), a program funded by the Bureau of Health Care Delivery and Assistance to train doctors. The distribution of assistance functioned much like a conditional scholarship to go to medical school. Through NHSC, the federal government paid for a recipient to attend their medical school of choice or where they were accepted on the condition that upon completion of study, they would serve the government for at least two years for each subsidized year. Ideally, the time owed was served before settling into practice. NHSC was having trouble with minority compliance. The students in question borrowed the most money and seemed to have the greatest difficulty paying it back by the agreed time. When Dr. Manley assumed the directorship, a number of the young physicians in trouble with the federal government were minority doctors, many of them from her alma mater Meharry.

It was unclear to her if they were behind in payments due to an eagerness to start private practice, or envisioned making enough money in sufficient time to reimburse the Corps, or any other possible line of thinking. Whatever the reasons, she inherited a backlog of files on young doctors who needed to reconcile their failed commitments.

> It just amazed me. It takes a good five years to just get on your feet in a medical practice. If you start out in debt, it takes longer than that. But they acquired all the trappings of wealth—big car, big house, vacations in the Bahamas, and all of that—and then filed bankruptcy.[9]

She visited nearly every applicable college campus in efforts to get medical students to understand the seriousness of their obligation. It was stressed that if the time was not paid back, interest accrued on the base amount of money provided. A year leave or deferment was possible, an option many of them were unaware of. She learned that the general thinking was as speculated and that one day they would be in a financial position to pay it off. The degree to which many of the young medical school graduates did, in fact, think doctors became rich essentially overnight was confirmed, a belief based on their perception of doctors they had seen, all of whom had money, fancy cars, and large homes. It was obvious to her they did not realize the physicians they observed had devoted years toward becoming established before they began making money; that their initial years entailed getting settled, investing in the future of a professional practice (putting out money) and hoping to be able to pay bills including their debt. She devoted a year to traveling where there were medical students, holding seminars and talking about medical school debt. The job was important to her and personal from the standpoint of dealing with so many Meharry graduates.

She recalled how before that, earlier in her career, she was on an admissions committee. Her grave concern was that African Americans were not getting into medical school and she wondered why. Taking on the self-appointed task of meticulously going through a deluge of applications was an admirable but almost nightmarish undertaking. She stated:

> It almost killed me. All of those applications. I had to carefully read every one of them. I had to attend the committee meetings and hear all the discussions, then fight for an occasional one that I had come across with obvious promise. I would tell them, 'Hey, we ought to give this young person a chance. I think he will make it.' While I was in the National Health Service Corps, I tried to bring awareness to that because it was a fully paid opportunity. But, of course, the government was owed years back for having trained you.[10]

From 1987 to 1989, while she worked on a loan repayment program, Dr. Manley appealed to US surgeon general Dr. Charles (C.) Everett Koop on behalf of Black officers. From the time Dr. Koop was sworn in on November 17, 1981, he wore the surgeon general's uniform, which was similar to that of a rear admiral in the Navy. He believed the uniform helped restore morale to the Commissioned Corps of the USPHS affected by cut-backs and PHS hospital closings in preceding years.

He instructed USPHS Commissioned Corps personnel to wear their uniforms so that he could recognize his officers.[11] White Corps members were equipped to quickly comply. African American members complained that they did not because they were not issued uniforms, and therefore, did not know the ranks of those among them.

Dr. Manley got on Dr. Koop's calendar to discuss problems in the agency. They determined that an advisory group would be beneficial but that there were too many committees already. It was not feasible to establish any more. Under the leadership of Rear Admiral (RADM) Audrey Manley, the entity that was unofficially called the Black Commissioned Officers Steering Committee, formed out of a delegation of officers who attended the 1987 meeting of the Congressional Black Caucus Health Braintrust, was formally organized as the Black Commissioned Officers Advisory Group (BCOAG).[12] The group developed a report of recommendations and initiatives for consideration by Dr. Koop. Black officers received Corps uniforms, were able to carry the nation's flag in ceremonies, sing in Corps groups, and participate in other duties and activities.

The Minority Officers Liaison Council (MOLC) was also established under Dr. Manley's oversight in 1989 to advise and serve the Office of the Surgeon General on issues of professional development and to advocate for the recognition of contributions made by minority officers in the USPHS. The MOLC was composed of four Chartered Minority Advisory Groups: American Indian/Alaska Native Commissioned Officers Advisory Committee (AIANCOAC); Asian Pacific American Officers Committee (APAOC); BCOAG; and Hispanic Officers Advisory Committee (HOAC).

While serving as the first minority woman to reach flag officer rank in the PHS, Dr. Manley discerned another shift in the path before her. She realized things were falling into place for her in ways far beyond her control—a divine intervention that positioned her for greater achievement. Things came seamlessly together as she approached her second year directing the NHSC. She realized the job would continue indefinitely with no change in issues. Getting the default numbers down and getting the doctors out of trouble was a challenge she effectively addressed. With a workable procedure in place, anyone could execute it. At about the precise moment that she began to look around for the next opportunity, the deputy assistant secretary for minority health abruptly left the position. Giving no warning or indication why to anyone, including Dr. Manley who knew her, the doctor simply walked out. It occurred to

Dr. Manley right away that she could do the job easily since it encompassed things she had already been doing. The position would allow her to remain in touch with sickle cell and genetics programs in addition to the NHSC where many of the medical staff were minority doctors.

She put a package together and sent it forward. The position had to be cleared by the assistant secretary of health (ASH). Dr. James Ostermann Mason, former director of the CDC, was the newly appointed ASH on his way to Washington from Atlanta. He was a well-known public health physician originally from Utah where he had served as director of the state health office prior to taking the lead post at CDC. Her packet landed on Dr. Mason's desk just before he arrived. Three days later, she received a call from him requesting a luncheon meeting in the dining hall in the basement of the Senate Office Building. He explained: "I'm making a series of meetings right now. I'm going to meet with Senator (Orrin) Hatch and I want to see you before I go." She did not know exactly where the Senate Office Building was, never having had an occasion to go downtown, but agreed to meet him there.

Dr. Mason exhibited a matter-of-fact manner from the onset of their interaction. He obviously was not someone who wasted time. Right away during lunch, he went straight to the point, stating: "I got your package and I want you to be my deputy." His words hit her like a lightning bolt—they were totally unexpected. He offered her the principal deputy assistant secretary of health (P-DASH) position, above the deputy assistant secretary for minority health opening for which she had applied. Dr. Manley had heard things about him, that he was tough, hard to get along with, did not take any stuff, and mostly that "he is not coming from Utah for nothing." In light of her original pursuit of the recently vacated minority health post, his statement caught her completely off guard. For the first time in her career, she was stunned, speechless, and wondered if he truly realized what he was saying. Noticing her reaction, he assured her, "Don't worry, you're going to be just fine."

Dr. Manly left the Senate Office Building and took a taxi back to the parking lot where she left her car. She made her way out of the Senate Office Building in search of a taxi the familiar parking lot where she left her car. The drive from the lot back to the office and then to home was a blur as her mind tried repeatedly to process what happened.

The next day, Dr. Mason called again, instructing her to take her information package to Mr. Ron Kaufman at the White House personnel office. He further informed her, "You cannot mention this to anybody. The new secretary is coming to Washington. Dr. Louis Sullivan will be here next week. You cannot tell anybody because Dr. Sullivan is going to have a press conference to announce your appointment." Assuring him she would not discuss what transpired with anyone, he then asked, "How are your Republican credentials?" She admitted, "Well, I don't have any, but my husband does." He seemed fine with that.

Her response referred to the strong historic relationship between the Rockefeller family and Spelman College. The philanthropic legacy alone was enough, with the college's name being derived from Mrs. Rockefeller's maiden name (Laura Spelman); Sisters Chapel being named for sisters Lucy and Laura Spelman through their estates; the Rockefeller name being honored on two buildings on campus; and a Rockefeller family member having been a fixture on the Spelman College Board of Trustees. As a Spelman alumna and former Spelman first lady, she felt a personal connectivity through the Rockefeller legacy, even though she anticipated the confusion that might surface among friends and former associates who saw her as "a good street Democrat for the people." Another important connection was the friendship and mutual regard that existed between her and Dr. Sullivan dating back to their undergraduate years as biochemistry classmates at Morehouse. It seemed as if she was covered.

Confident the process would go smoothly, she found her way to the White House personnel office, went inside, and interacted briefly with a young woman at the front desk who told her to place the package in an inbox, commenting: "I'll give it to Dr. Kaufman." Dr. Manley responded politely, "Okay. Thank you," and walked away. She exited the building, made it to the end of the block, and was waiting at a red light when the young lady ran up behind her calling, "Dr. Manley. Dr. Manley. Wait a minute. Wait a minute." Gaining her attention, the woman waved the paperwork toward her and asked, "Have you done all of this?" When Dr. Manley answered, "Yes, that's my CV," the young lady said, "Mr. Kaufman wants to meet you. So will you come back?" Dr. Manley said, "Yes, I'll come back." She returned to the office and met with Ron Kaufman for half an hour.

Bound to secrecy regarding the upcoming position change, her boss remained Rear Admiral Ed Martin until the new title was confirmed and announced. She was scheduled to travel to Mississippi to speak at the Jackson-Hinds Neighborhood Health Center at a luncheon on the upcoming Friday, the same day as the planned Sullivan press conference in Washington, DC. The neighborhood center in Jackson was one of their funded programs. She and Dr. Martin were supposed to meet there so that he could introduce her. Following instructions regarding the impending announcement, she remained in Washington instead. On Thursday night her phone rang. A concerned Dr. Martin bluntly asked, "Where are you?"

She was uncertain about how to respond, yet managed to get out, “I am still in DC. I have had an unfortunate experience. I’m not going to be able to get there. You’re going to have to cover for me.” She knew the story did not wash but felt there was nothing else she could say or do. She had stepped out on faith and the desire of her heart was delivered. It was 1989.

CHAPTER 10

Moving Up Downtown

On March 1, 1989, Dr. Louis Wade Sullivan was sworn in as secretary of the HHS. In May, he announced the appointment of Dr. Audrey Forbes Manley as principal deputy assistant secretary of health (P-DASH) under Dr. James Mason. Meanwhile, on that day, Dr. Martin amused the crowd in Jackson, Mississippi, which had gathered to hear Dr. Manley speak by explaining her absence with the true anecdote: "I left Washington yesterday and I was her boss. When I go back, she will be my boss." Events transpired so rapidly that Dr. Manley confessed to initially being "a little scared to death" with the new development. Prior to Dr. Sullivan's press conference, a team arrived, packed her entire office in the Parklawn Building, loaded everything into a car, and transported the boxes and her downtown for the announcement.

According to her, the press release alone drew out the usual Washington nay-sayers she determined to be in this particular case, mostly White men envious of a Black woman who had advanced. Their negativity and prejudice were not new to her as they spread presumptive comments such as: "She is not going to make it in that position. She's in over her head. She can't deal with downtown. They are going to eat her alive." Furthermore, if you were not in uniform every day, there was a lack of understanding of the nature of your connection in the system for many people. Since she wore civilian clothes, most observers did not realize she had flag rank.[1]

In actuality, there was no real adjustment period or time to be affected by such idle comments. At three o'clock that afternoon, Dr. Mason notified her that he and Dr. Sullivan were heading to Geneva, Switzerland, very soon for a World Health Organization (WHO) meeting. For the second instance in a relatively short period of time, he caught her off guard. stating, "Now, I know I just pulled you down here. And if you don't want to be acting, I can name someone else. It is a lot. If you don't want me to do that, I won't." She realized the responsibility it entailed, but also recognized the breadth of implications as a woman and an African American. There was the additional awareness that if someone else was allowed to serve as acting because she took a pass, the option for her to advance may never present itself in the future. Everyone had to know she was in charge while Dr. Mason was away and that she was capable of doing the job. So, she told him in a definite tone, yes, she would handle it.

Dr. Manley was introduced to consultant Dr. Jim Dixon, a troubleshooter who put out fires when something was going on. He was a company man who did not belong to a political party and had impressive credentials. It would not have been out of the realm of possibility or acceptability if Dr. Mason had asked Dr. Dixon to assume the acting role given her recent arrival and the nature of things in Washington. However, proceeding as he did, Dr. Mason not only confirmed he trusted her abilities, it showed respect for her position as principal deputy assistant, third in line after the secretary. She decided to take the opportunity to underscore the fact, if not outright prove, that a woman could run an office in such a predominantly male setting. With Dr. Mason and Dr. Sullivan in Geneva, she was acting assistant secretary of health during her first two weeks on the job, and as such, her responsibilities temporarily quadrupled.

As P-DASH, she had a large suite of offices and managed to pull in the named staff she pretty much wanted. That included Patty Dean, the secretary who had been with her from day one at Maternal and Child Health at HRSA, ending the speculation that she would end up downtown alone. Captain Steve Moore was the special assistant responsible for making sure her wishes were carried out to desired specifications and standards. She sat in the office located next to the doctor who had purview over the entire PHS system. She communicated directly with officers at agencies whose staffs totaled thirty-five to forty thousand people, and represented the office when Dr. Mason could not or chose not to participate in official matters. Dr. Mason maximized the benefits of having Dr. Manley as a member of his team. She was acknowledged by the National Medical Association (NMA) and the American Medical Association (AMA), regarded highly by Dr. David Satcher and Dr. Louis Sullivan, who was the President of Morehouse School of Medicine when he wrote her letter of recommendation, and recognized her breadth of expertise of national public health, medical care matters relative to diverse communities, and African American physicians in a range of specialties.

She often accompanied Dr. Mason to meetings, sitting in as an extra pair of eyes and ears, or in case something came up that he needed information about. Typically, at each meeting's conclusion, he would turn to her and ask, "Now, what do you think?" Their discussion usually culminated with her expressing an idea about one issue or another, or her recommendation for handling a covered problem, to which he would tell her, "Okay, let's do it."

One of the earliest tasks assigned to her was organizing the official dinner welcoming Dr. Sullivan to Washington, DC, in his cabinet position. Dr. Mason gave the responsibility to her. She, in turn, solicited assistance from members of the BCOAG. The affair was held at the Navy Officers' Club located on the Bethesda campus across from the National Institute of Health. On the evening of the event, as the dinner was well underway, Dr. Mason suddenly stood and said to those gathered, "Just a minute, I have something to say." Dr. Manley questioned in her mind what he could possibly be doing, since he was not on the agenda at that point. Dr. Mason then instructed her, "Dr. Manley, I want you to come up here." She was puzzled and felt unprepared for whatever he had imposed on the festivity but made her way quickly to the speaker's table. At that moment, he announced, "Dr. Manley, you are no longer an O-7; you are now an O-8." In addition to being a gesture of welcome to Dr. Sullivan, it was the night of her promotion. Dr. Mason had totally surprised her for a third time. She was the go-to person when Dr. Mason wanted to pull anything off, but in this case, he obviously entrusted someone else to get it done, and without her having the slightest clue. As she indulged in the excitement of the moment, she noticed a heart-warming sight—Dr. Albert Manley stood beaming, literally grinning from ear to ear.

The new rank gave her a second star and the highest grade for a career officer. With the news, a reception was planned in her honor. It was held at the Cosmos Club, where Dr. Albert Manley, Dr. Jim Cheek, and, according to her, "all the boys" had membership.[2] Everything was taken care of down to the most meticulous details by Captain Moore, her young special assistant who was a logistical fixture by her side. Captain Moore had quickly learned what her likes and preferences were, and anything planned by or for her was carried out by him to perfection. The reception drew more than a hundred guests from around the country, including Dr. Johnnetta B. Cole and her (then) husband, Arthur James Robinson, Jr., from Atlanta; friends from New York; several Washington dignitaries; family; and many young Black officers in uniform who were thrilled to see an African

American woman achieve the rank. It was a high-profile acknowledgment of her promotion and work performance.

As P-Dash, she "cut her teeth on the AIDS epidemic." The disease was on the forefront of national public health concerns when Dr. Koop was US surgeon general.[3] Dr. Koop emphasized public education on prevention and protection, was opposed to both mandatory testing and quarantine of the infected, and denounced discrimination against sufferers in schools, at work, and in housing. He represented the US at international health meetings, including those at the WHO where concerns about the AIDS epidemic were increasing.

Concerns about the global threat of the virus escalated just as she was settling downtown to work with Dr. Mason. Their first act was organizing a working conference to discuss the ongoing AIDS threat. She and Dr. Mason outlined the scope of the problem and projected the resources that would be needed to combat the AIDS epidemic. They held a three-day retreat in West Virginia, and in usual manner, broke out into five work groups. The meetings included scientists such as Dr. (Anthony) Tony Stephen Fauci, director of the National Institute of Allergy and Infectious Diseases, professionals from the Centers for Disease Control and Prevention, and specialists from the NHSC and physicians.

Dr. Manley led the group charged with estimating the cost to the PHS, in particular, and the federal government overall to combat AIDS. When Dr. Manley reported back to the meeting representing her group indicating the funds that would be needed to fight the disease was roughly sixteen billion dollars ($16 billion), most members of the other groups wanted to "crucify her." They were more than upset, they were in utter disbelief. Several participants interrupted her with harsh statements and sharp protests. The most audible comment was: "How dare you come up with a figure like that!" Only one person came to her defense. Dr. June E. Osborn, an infectious disease specialist (epidemiologist) and Dean of the School of Public Health at the University of Michigan rose and interjected a-matter-of-factly: "This number is not unrealistic. As a matter of fact, the cost may be even more than that." When she spoke, Dr. Osborn restored order to the gathering in such a way that Dr. Manley was able to continue and explain the basis for the group's tabulation.

The report informed the body that addressing AIDS effectively was a multilayered process. It was contingent on educating nurses, physicians and ancillary health personnel; providing information that would change textbooks in medical and nursing schools; changing educational training for residents and doctors who were graduating; and the greatest challenge, informing doctors already practicing medicine, seeing patients, and being unaware of what was coming through the door. Each component of the necessary procedure had to be costed out, along with the number of years it would likely take to get on top of the disease.

> If it's a billion dollars in two years—considering you are talking about eight years—you are still dealing with AIDS. We had to look at it in the long run. It was projecting where the AIDS epidemic was going to go, and we did not have the vaccine yet. We were dealing with people who were going to die.[4]

Dr. Manley was the point person for curricula development and setting up educational facilities and materials across the spectrum of health care providers for the office. They did not have to do all the hands-on work, but secured funds for continuing education, facilities upgrading, research, and support for Dr. Fauci at NIH and for CDC.

Once there was an AIDS test to determine the presence of the virus, a battle ensued between American and French research laboratories. The dispute began in 1984 over who first discovered that AIDS was caused by HIV. It unfolded between Dr. Robert Gallo, head of the AIDS lab at the National Cancer Institute (NCI) in the US, and the Pasteur Institute in France led by Luc Montagnier. The battle over who should get credit was detrimental to ongoing research.

Mutual interest in moving forward made having serious discussions necessary about approaches amenable to both nations. Dr. Manley led an American delegation sent to Paris in 1987 to work with representatives from the Pasteur Institute on a possible resolution. With bottom-line issues having much to do with patents which translated into revenue as well as recognition, the two sides formed a joint agreement where Gallo and Montagnier shared credit for the discovery, and they along with their respective governments would share patent royalties.[5] They further agreed that money from sales of the vaccine would be used to fund research. A Joint National Institute of Health/Pasteur Institute Grant Review Panel was established charged with conducting annual assessments of research proposals during an event held in the two countries on an alternating basis. Dr. Manley was the US panelist at the first NIH/Pasteur Institute Grant Review when it convened in Paris, submitting to the daunting task of reviewing and writing up a sizeable number of grant applications, while fighting urges to break out and visit the Champs-Elysees and other sites in the city she grew to love.

Back in the US, a minority-related matter emerged that required her particular attention. She learned that Meharry was in severe financial trouble, about to go bankrupt. Dr. David Satcher had assumed the presidency at the college without full knowledge of the serious level of its financial problems.[6] A candid briefing from Dr. Sullivan alerted Dr. Mason of the situation, and he, in turn, passed the information on to her, stating: "Dr. Sullivan cannot serve as secretary and see Meharry shut down. He has already candidly stated he is not going to be the secretary while Meharry has to close its doors. What can we do?" Without hesitation, her answer was, "Dr. Mason, don't worry about it. I'll take care of it."

She became chair of the PHS Task Force on Meharry and began by composing a Memorandum of Understanding (MOU) between the PHS and Meharry Medical College. Drawing from fundamental strategies that had been successful in the past, she established the necessary procedures, put a work group together, identified and earmarked resources, and had a legal document created outlining the agency's plan of action to assist. A priority was the institution's need for a viable medical facility. Meharry's Hubbard Hospital was small, dated, in need of renovation, and had a shortage of bed space for patients, which minimized its effectiveness as a good teaching hospital.

Dr. Manley drew inspiration from the model she established at Grady Hospital in Atlanta to form the plan of action. Aware that federal money was allocated to the state of Tennessee for Vanderbilt to administer care to the city's lower income populations at Nashville General Hospital, she questioned why Meharry was not participating. She worked with both institutions to achieve a different, cooperative arrangement. The agency agreed to facilitate Meharry reaching a point of sufficiency to join Vanderbilt University in administering care at Nashville General. The ultimate goal was for Vanderbilt to gradually turn over sole management of the hospital to Meharry.[7] This was ideal for both schools since Vanderbilt wanted to get out of Nashville General in order to focus on satellite facilities serving the increasing number of suburban communities.

NHSC physicians were assigned to assist Meharry.[8] Progress was monitored. Meharry Medical College Board of Trustees Chairman Dr. Frank S. Royal, Sr., and President Satcher had routine conference calls, initially twice a month, then monthly. Dr. Manley was in direct communication with Dr. Satcher on a weekly basis. Eventually, the financial support that came into the state was channeled to Meharry to run Nashville General across town. Her strategy worked. The medical college was saved.

In August 1992, while Dr. Mason and Dr. Sullivan attended a WHO summit in Geneva once again, weather forecasters accurately predicted that a severe tropical storm in the Atlantic off the Florida coast would intensify. The storm soon reached hurricane wind strength and became Hurricane Andrew. After initial PHS meetings were held in the threatened region (IV), and the agency's Office of Emergency Preparedness established a hurricane watch, Dr. Manley, as acting assistant secretary for health, was briefed. The next day, Monday, August 24 at 5:00 am (Eastern Daylight Time), category 5 Hurricane Andrew made landfall in south Dade County, Florida, with maximum sustained winds of 165 mph and a minimum central pressure of 922 mbar. The storm left a trail of destruction across Dade, Monroe, and Broward Counties. The storm entered the Gulf of Mexico and turned north to strike land again two days later at Cypremort Point near Morgan City, Louisiana, at 4:00 am (Central Daylight Time).

Dr. Manley remembered:

> I'll never forget the evening because I had left the disaster center and gone home for a little while. Preparing to come back, the telephone rang. I was upstairs trying to get downstairs to the phone when I slipped, fell on the stairs, and discovered later I had broken my coccyx.

With the Florida hit, there was immediate recognition that this storm was different.

President George H. W. Bush declared both locations federal disaster areas. The damage to Louisiana was significant but not nearly as catastrophic as that suffered in the densely populated areas in southern Dade County, Florida. Hurricane Andrew was the most expensive natural disaster in US history at the time, leaving a trail of damage totaling roughly $26.5 billion.[9] It was the first major hurricane to strike the Florida peninsula in more than twenty-five years.[10] PHS had the lead federal government role in making sure the public health and medical care needs were met with the Federal Emergency Management Agency (FEMA) as the coordinating entity.

The PHS was seldom the subject of news coverage in terms of their operation and responsibilities of the service, but Hurricane Andrew was so destructive, this case was different. Typically, PHS would preposition manpower, and materials for the disaster area, wait until the disaster has passed, and then move in. The plan for this storm was to preposition at Homestead Air Force Base, some distance from Miami airport, where there was a hospital and everything needed. It turned out Homestead, Florida was the hardest-hit community with almost one hundred percent of the mobile homes completely destroyed. The hurricane hit Homestead Air Force Base and disabled the hospital, making it necessary for a new response to be created. They decided to fly into Opa-locka in the northern part of the state, and transport supplies and equipment south to the Miami area by truck. Local police and state troopers were strictly enforcing movement of traffic into and out of the Miami area, prohibiting their trucks from getting through. They eventually managed to get response teams to the Miami-Dade Air Force hanger, which was their base of operation.

For the duration of the recovery period, FEMA and the PHS maintained twenty-four-hour Emergency Operations Centers to ensure field and support personnel were able to obtain necessary supplies and equipment to perform their assignments. Throughout the emergency response phase, PHS deployed sixteen disaster medical assistance teams (DMATs) of 460 personnel who treated 17,290 patients. As relief efforts were making inroads toward recovery, Dr. Manley determined: "We had never had a disaster that major. It was at that point that we knew there had to be discussions about global warming, natural disasters, and their increase in frequency and severity. Hurricane Andrew was the first one. We knew others were likely coming."

Dealing with the aftermath of the hurricane clarified for her the degree to which they were ill-prepared for major disasters. She realized that the roughly six small units set up throughout the country were not enough to handle weather phenomena of the magnitude of Hurricane Andrew. She pulled the various work groups together to determine all that was required to cover such a disaster and organized the information in a comprehensive and detailed report. Noticing the increase in frequency and severity of natural disasters, Dr. Manley concluded there was an urgent need for a different federal plan of preparedness and response. The report included, among other points, recommendations for how PHS would provide health care and manpower, the Department of Defense would provide transportation, and FEMA would remain the managerial body. The report led to the establishment of the Commission Corps Readiness Force (CCRF) and the National Training Conference on Commission Corps Readiness designed to improve the HHS' ability to respond to public health emergencies.[11]

The document also made it clear that, going forward, there would be more extensive training for commissioned officers. There were available nurses, doctors, physical therapists, and sanitation specialists, many in the Federal Health System. They were the Army, Marines, Navy, Air Force, Coast Guard, PHS Commissioned Corps, and National Oceanic and Atmospheric Administration.

The report detailed the roles, responsibilities, and procedures for moving on the part of the doctors, nurses, and sanitariums, depending on the disaster. In her assessment, it was reasonable and logical that those entities responsible for responding should be trained properly.

As P-DASH, another responsibility was serving as a member of the US Delegation to United Nations Children's Fund (UNICEF) and the UNICEF/WHO Joint Committee on Health Policy (JCHP) from 1990 to 1993. This required overseas travel to board and committee meetings. Mandatory trips out of the country as P-DASH were so demanding she assessed they were "enough to kill you in and of themselves." Notwithstanding high-profile oversight of issues that emerged and the physical pressures endured, she assisted in directing the eight agencies and eighteen ASH and PHS program and staff offices under their jurisdiction.

The months leading up to the completion of her four-year mark on the job were approaching. Threats from the AIDS virus and accelerating natural disasters were more effectively on national and global action radars. Meharry was on course toward financial stability. Without compromising domestic tasks, US presence, participation, and leadership in international health matters remained positions of strength and effectiveness. At this juncture, Washington, DC, and the nation were thrust into a climate of vigorous political activity. It was a presidential election year with the usual high stakes for professionals in appointed positions.

On Tuesday evening November 3, 1992, Democratic Arkansas Governor William (Bill) Jefferson Clinton defeated incumbent Republican President George H. W. Bush, Independent businessman Ross Perot of Texas, and a number of minor candidates in the general election to become president-elect of the US. As usual, those individuals who held cabinet seats and other high-ranking positions appointed by the out-going administration wasted no time in making preparations to vacate their offices. Dr. Sullivan and Dr. Mason made arrangements for their exits while Dr. Manley, essentially in limbo, prepared for the new group to come in. President-Elect Clinton nominated Dr. Donna Edna Shalala for US secretary of health and human services pending Senate confirmation after his inaugural. Dr. Manley was asked to serve in an acting capacity as ASH until a nominee was selected. This meant she sat temporarily on title, including on the Intergovernmental Affairs slot during the transition, and continued to do the necessary day-to-day work of the bureau as P-DASH. It was 1992.

CHAPTER 11

Facing Destiny in Washington, DC

President William Jefferson Clinton was sworn in as the forty-second president of the US on Wednesday, January 20, 1993, at the West Front of the US Capital in Washington, DC. Two days later, on January 22, the Senate voted to confirm Dr. Donna Edna Shalala as the HHS secretary. For a second time, Dr. Manley worked for the new secretary who she knew personally from her AUC days—Dr. Shalala, having served on the Spelman College Board of Trustees. Amid speculation, possibly hope, that she would be "kicked out" once the secretary was in place, Dr. Manley remained in her position. Male observers, in particular, could not understand her survival, and openly inquired, "how do you manage to stay down there?" They were left to ponder the question for themselves.

Before the end of the month, President Clinton announced Dr. (Minnie) Joycelyn Elders was his choice to serve as the next US surgeon general. The appointment made her the first African American and second woman to hold the position, after Dr. Antonia Coello Novello during the Bush administration (1990–1993). Dr. Elders was not confirmed until September 7, but upon the announcement, Dr. Manley went into help mode. She was still acting ASH and waiting for her own next assignment. To her, it was not only decent, it was the professional thing to do, explaining:

> When Dr. Elders came in it was just natural that I would extend a hand and offer her all the help that I could. I had been around for almost 20 years. I knew where all the bodies were buried; where the dangerous pitfalls were located; and who the people were that would dig ditches for her to fall into. I was familiar with all those potential hidden dangers. Most of all, I was an old hand who was a career person with no political ambition.[1]

In the fall, about the time Dr. Elders received Senate approval, Dr. Philip Randolph Lee was named the HHS' assistant secretary for health for a second time. He had served as ASH under President Lyndon B. Johnson from 1965 to 1969. His appointment ended the need for Dr. Manley to hold down the acting position. The professional synergy and regard that had formed between her and Dr. Elder resulted in the surgeon general asking Dr. Manley to become her deputy effective January 1994. Dr. Manley accepted. The deputy surgeon general title marked another unprecedented development in Dr. Manley's career. It was the first occasion when a senior administrative health professional transitioned from a Republican to a Democratic administration and remained in the leadership circle of the PHS.

The opportunity was neither expected nor taken lightly:

> I learned a lot from that, because usually when one political group leaves and the incoming leadership is of the other political persuasion, everybody stands back, throws up their hands, and do [sic] nothing, waiting to see which way the wind is going to blow. Sometimes they play tricks. Often you hear stories passed around about how something is going awry, meaning somebody probably 'planned a little party for them.' Of course, I was not like that and I was not the only one. Career people in general are not like that; they go from one administration to the next without a problem. We are not political. We do not vote. That is why we have the Hatch Act. Government employees are called 'hatched.' We are not supposed to contribute to political parties. We work equally well for Democrats and Republicans.[2]

Historically, her career record in Washington was one of diligence, commitment, and over and above the call of duty when it came to work.

When Dr. Mason chose her to be his deputy in 1989, the position in the Office of Minority Health (OMH) that she had actually applied for remained vacant. The position was established under President George H. Bush as part of Surgeon General Koop's revitalization of the Commission Corps strictly for Minority Health. Since the post was unmanned, she took care of all responsibilities that fell under the office so that Dr. Mason did not have to worry about them.

Dr. Manley held down two forts, serving as P-DASH by title and serving as the titular head of the Minority Health office. It turned out that her propensity for wearing multiple hats was no different during the next administration. From 1994 to 1995, her duties as deputy surgeon general were compounded by the official responsibility of those of acting deputy assistant secretary for minority health by title. At this point, in the fulfillment of both assignments, she devoted half of each day in one office location and the remainder of the day in the other.

Helping the new team of leaders settle in without stepping on any minefields, directing a department where people are worried about hot spots that were not covered, and attending to Minority Health responsibilities was an unbelievably tough load to carry. Over time, she had to admit the work was excessive and taking a heavy toll, literally wearing her down. After considerable thought about putting someone in place who could do what needed to be done, Dr. Clay E. Simpson, Jr., MSPH, PhD, came to mind as an ideal person to fulfill the mission of the OMH. Dr. Clay Simpson was the only minority male at the time in a supervisory position in HRSA. He had the educational background, professional experience, and ability to deliver respectable services for minority people.

Dr. Simpson had been with the agency for a number of years directing the Division of Disadvantaged Assistance in HRSA. As an established figure in the trenches of the agency, he was reluctant to leave the division where there was safety and security to take a move up that could be affected when the administration changed. It was a sentiment shared by many career people who were afraid to take the risk of assuming a higher job title because it changed them from being career to becoming political. Getting Dr. Simpson into the position was a major accomplishment. It took a great deal of persuasion to convince him to take the position. His acceptance and willingness to begin in January 1995 could not have been timelier.

Dr. Elders was forced to resign effective December 31, 1994, amid controversy resulting from her outspoken views about drugs and sexuality.[3] In the interim, Dr. Manley was named acting surgeon general by law. No deputy was appointed, as was usual practice. She assumed the leadership position while still remaining deputy. As principal federal spokesperson to the Nation on matters of public health and medicine, she was special advisor to the president, the Congress and the general population on hazards to health, disease prevention, and health promotion. Among the several programs, initiatives, and interests managed, the entities she interfaced with as the responsible person for the development, release, and distribution of scientifically based review publications on critical health topics were the FEMA, Environmental Protection Agency (EPA), Department of Transportation (DOT), Justice Department (DOJ), State Department (DOS), and Commerce Department (DOC).

For an unprecedented two-and-a-half years, no one came behind her and covered the deputy surgeon general position. She was forced to do both. Release from oversight of the OMH at the onset of her acting surgeon general role was, from her perspective, a blessing. Filling the surgeon general position was not an easy process for the Clinton administration. After a nominee was identified, their name was passed on for Senate approval. There was more than one effort made to get a physician confirmed that the administration was not politically able to pull off. Dr. David Satcher, former president of Meharry Medical College, was then director of the CDC in Atlanta. His name was put forth to the president as a viable choice for appointment as the next US surgeon general.

A member of Phi Beta Kappa, Dr. Satcher attended Morehouse College and became the first African American to earn both the MD and PhD from Case Western Reserve University. He completed his Internship and Residency at the University of Rochester's Strong Memorial Hospital in 1972, and relocated to Los Angeles, California, to begin his medical career as the Macy Foundation Fellow in community medicine at King-Drew Medical Center. Over the next decade, Dr. Satcher held concurrent administrative and teaching positions. He was director of the King-Drew Sickle Cell Research Center for six years; medical director at the Second Baptist Free Clinic (1974–1979); faculty member at the UCLA School of Medicine and Public Health; and while interim dean of the Charles R. Drew Postgraduate Medical School (1977–1979), he negotiated the agreement with the UCLA School of Medicine and the Board of Regents that led to a medical education program at King-Drew. In 1979, Dr. Satcher returned to Atlanta to serve as professor and Chairman of the Department of Community Medicine and Family Practice at Morehouse School of Medicine. He went on to assume the presidency at Meharry Medical College (1982–1993) and, in 1994, was named director of the CDC in Atlanta.

Once he came to the attention of President Clinton as a strong candidate for the appointment of surgeon general that would likely gain approval, Dr. Satcher did not wait for confirmation before encouraging the president to do something for Tuskegee related to the Tuskegee Experiment. Dr. Satcher was the driving force behind a plan of action that addressed the mistreatment of African American male residents of Macon Country, Alabama who were enrolled in a PHS project, expecting to receive medical care but were subjected to the untreated observation of syphilis progression instead. The delusion and lack of medical attention led to severe health problems for the participants, including blindness, mental impairment, and death. Dr. Satcher's efforts were the impetus for a historic event where President Clinton publicly acknowledged the betrayal that had occurred and took measures to begin a public healing process.

President Bill Clinton, on May 16, 1997, issued a formal apology for The Tuskegee Study of Untreated Syphilis in the Negro Male, commonly referred to as the Tuskegee Experiment. Conducted at Tuskegee Institute (now Tuskegee University) under the auspices of the US PHS with a projected six-month timeline, the study actually lasted forty years—from 1932 until 1972. The duration made it "the longest nontherapeutic experiment on human beings in the history of medicine and public health."[4]

Five of the eight survivors were in attendance: Herman Shaw (ninety-four) who introduced President Clinton, Charlie Pollard (ninety-one), Carter Howard (ninety-three), Frederick Moss (in his nineties), and Fred Simmons, who estimated his age at 110. Gwendolyn Cox, daughter of Sam Doner, and Christopher Monroe, grandson of George Key, attended on behalf of their respective relatives. North Hendon was present, representing his brother Ernest Hendon who was unable to travel and watched via satellite from Tuskegee. Dr. Satcher, the leader of the effort, and Vice President Al Gore stood with the president as a show of solidarity and support of his actions.

In her continued capacity as acting surgeon general, Dr. Manley was sent to Tuskegee to represent the White House during the satellite broadcast. She witnessed the ceremony in the company of families, community leaders, teachers, and students who lived, worked, and studied in the environment where violations had occurred, painful memories were prevalent, and the mistrust of governmental motives ran deep. President Clinton's statement included the announcement of the award of a $200,000 grant to assist in the establishment of a center for bioethics in research and healthcare at Tuskegee University as part of a "lasting memorial" to the study's victims.[5]

Dr. Manley recalled the impact of the president's words on the Tuskegee, Alabama gathering:

> It (the apology) was so very important to occur. It was also important to be in Tuskegee as the voice of the White House. They had a conference call, videos came in, and it was as if we were all together. Initiating the Ethics Center had a huge positive effect. The impact was immediate. Establishment of the Center for Ethical Medicine was considered necessary to ensure something like that *would never happen again.*[6]

Offering startup funds for the formation of the National Center for Bioethics in Research and Health Care, the first of its kind in the nation, drew the following statement from Tuskegee University President Dr. Benjamin F. Payton:

> The launching of this Center marks a turning point in a history plagued by abuse and abandonment, and we have the opportunity to address and ameliorate the terrible legacy of the U.S. Public Health Service Study... We are pleased to be able to play such an important role in this critical transition, and to continue the University's longstanding tradition of providing innovative health care solutions from an African American perspective.[7]

By statute, being in the acting position, Dr. Manley served on the Board of Regents for the National Library of Medicine, the largest national health library in the world located at the NIH. She sat on the Library's "Changing the Face of Medicine" committee, charged with providing snapshots of women in medicine as one approach to attracting and getting more women in the field. Being the more informed member of the committee about underrepresented women in medicine at the time, she shared the names of African American female doctors practicing in obscure places and cultural communities. These were people who were doing great jobs but because of race, NIH would not have picked them up.

The list she submitted identified physicians such as Dr. Grace Marilynn James, the first African American on the staff of the Louisville Children's Hospital and the faculty of the University of Louisville School of Medicine; Dr. Natalia Tanner, the first African American woman to be board certified in Detroit, Michigan, and first woman and African American to serve as president of the Michigan Chapter of the American Academy of Pediatrics; and Dr. Barbara Ross-Lee, the first African American woman dean of a US medical school—the College of Osteopathic Medicine of Ohio University in Athens, Ohio.

In her advisory role, Dr. Manley enhanced tremendously the presence of African American women whose achievements may have gone unknown. In fact, all of the initial names of Black physicians profiled came from her list. "Of course, 'Changing the face of Medicine' fell right in line with the things I saw coming and wanted preparation for at Spelman early on. I knew women would become more integral participants in medicine and Spelman graduates would be well represented because of the Black female emphasis there."

Among Dr. Manley's additional contributions in the acting role was bringing renewed attention to the status of physical health in adults and the need to include a conscious regimen of activity in lifestyles to improve and maintain overall wellness. Not exactly stating the obvious, the recommendations from such a high public health position did serve as a reminder of the historical interest that came out of the Oval Office over an extensive period of time. In June 1956, President Dwight David Eisenhower (1890–1969) created the President's Council on Youth Fitness with cabinet-level status which was intended to create public awareness of the need for improved fitness among America's youth. Later, President John F. Kennedy (1917–1963) changed the name to the President's Council on Physical Fitness to address all age groups and enlisted the aid of citizens, civic groups, organizations, etc., as partners to federal efforts. By the time President Lyndon Baines Johnson (1908–1973) was in office, he named it the President's Council on Physical Fitness and Sports to encourage lasting gains through ongoing participation in sports and athletic games.

During the Clinton administration, in 1996, Dr. Manley's office released the landmark *Physical Activity and Health: A Report of the Surgeon General*, the Office of the Surgeon General's first-ever report on physical activity and health. The report found that sixty percent of adults did not achieve the recommended amount of physical activity, and twenty-five percent of adults were not physically active at all. The 292-page document was deliberately released on the eve of the Centennial Olympic Games in Atlanta, Georgia.

Even though change was on the horizon, Dr. Manley kept operational matters in the office on track, making sure any potential problems were confronted in a timely manner. She was still running across the country, going to Geneva, and doing responsible work the position required. At the same time, she knew Dr. David Satcher was coming. They had prepared him well. His credentials were in order, and everything was set to go. As for herself, being a twenty-five-year veteran of federal professional service, including high level administration and twenty plus years of military rank; with a history of working in leadership in medical service and academic teaching for fifteen years, much had been accomplished due to her input, presence and participation. She found comfort in the thought of being away from it all, but had not decided what to do next, or if it was time to stop. Without pursuing anything, she concluded if something good came up, she would take it. If nothing came up, she would retire.

Destiny manifested itself again. Just as serious thought was given to her next move, she received a phone call at the office from a member of the Spelman College Board of Trustees indicating that president of Spelman, Dr. Johnnetta Cole, was stepping down. She was told they were putting together a search committee and wanted to know if they could talk to her. Her immediate reaction was, "Well, I don't know. What do you want to talk to me about?" Their response was, "Well, we just want to talk to you." At home that evening, she shared the conversation with her husband, stating, "Johnnetta is stepping down as president at Spelman and they want to talk to me. I don't know why. I'm a doctor. I'm not in education." Albert Manley told her, "Well, at least you ought to talk to them." When she asked, "You really think so?" he advised, "Yes, talk to them. You don't have to do anything, but at least you should talk to them." After considerable thought and encouragement from Albert, she notified Spelman officials of her willingness to meet.

When she met with the search committee in January, they emphasized the sciences, specifically how the increased number of majors created the need for a new science building. Tapley Hall, where she had studied as an undergraduate, was built in 1927 and had become inadequate. They needed a new science building. Bottom line, that was their sales pitch. Science.

Dr. Manley gave the offer serious thought briefly, then did not think about it at all. Still acting as surgeon general, He had so much work to do on that front, compounded by the impending transition of authority to Dr. Satcher, so for the time being, she let it go.

Soon the college made their case again. Dr. Etta Falconer made a personal and private trip to Manley's Washington home during the end of January to make a one-on-one appeal. Dr. Falconer was provost and longtime mathematics chair in what was, at the time, the Department of Math and Science. The two had worked together on projects and initiatives when Dr. Manley was First Lady, and had kept in touch professionally since Manley's departure in 1976. During the visit, they sat and talked on the living room couch as longtime friends. What affected Dr. Manley most was the look on Dr. Falconer's face when she commented, "We really need you to come back. We need a new science building. We need your help."

She knew where Dr. Falconer was coming from; knew how challenging things had been when on the campus twenty-five years earlier. Now, learning that thirty-seven percent of the young women at Spelman were in math and science, and already aware that a National Science Foundation survey determined that Spelman was the number two institution in the country placing African Americans in science and health-related fields, she needed to think about it.[8]

The second meeting with the search committee in early March offered a reiteration of science-related issues that had been presented before. Although grants and equipment were coming in to support the discipline, Tapley could not do the job. The campaign was an attention-retainer because of Dr. Manley's unwavering interest in women pursuing and excelling in healthcare and her longstanding belief that Spelman was positioned like no other institution to produce substantial future leadership in science among African American women. Once again, she committed to giving the offer consideration.

On the cusp of making a decision, there was a fateful sequence of events with origins dating back to 1987 and the arrival of Dr. Johnnetta B. Cole as president of Spelman. While in Atlanta on a business trip to CDC in her capacity as the Director of Genetic Services, Dr. Manley arranged a side visit to the college to meet the new president of her alma mater. When they met, Dr. Manley made her an offer: "We have a lovely home in Jamaica and I know you are going to need time to rest. So, whenever you want to go down there, just let us know. You are welcome to be our guest."[9]

For ten years Dr. Cole and her husband vacationed at the Manley home in Jamaica. Each time, with one exception, they had the home to themselves without Audrey and Albert Manley being there. Planning what turned out to be their final visit, Dr. Cole expressed interest in the four of them being on the island at the same time. In 1996, she said, "Next time, I want to visit while you and Albert are here. I want to go when we can all be together."[10] Dr. Manley agreed, "Okay, that's a good idea. My birthday is March 25th. Let's plan on going next year for my birthday. We will all go together." The agreement was set.

The two couples arranged to be together at the Manley vacation home, called Jayhawk, in Montego Bay, Jamaica for her birthday. Dr. Manley gave the following account of the course of events during their stay:

> We played golf every morning beginning at seven thirty, and came off the course around 9:30 or ten o'clock. That Friday morning, which was March the 26th, Albert and Johnnetta decided to stay at the house and swim. Art and I went to the golf course as usual.
>
> At the ninth hole, Arthur said to me, 'Have you made up your mind about Spelman yet? Do you know what you're going to do?' By now everybody knew I had met with the search committee. This was at 9:30 that morning. I said, 'I can't see it. I just cannot see it. I cannot see myself going back and dragging Albert back to Atlanta. I dragged him to DC kicking and screaming. He is really older now. I just can't see myself dragging him back to Atlanta where I know how unhappy he would be being on Spelman's campus and not being the president.'

> We went back to the house. We swam. Johnnetta and I were sitting on the veranda. The veranda overlooked the pool. Then, Albert had a heart attack in the swimming pool. We were sitting there, drinking our tea and talking, and I heard my name, 'Audrey! Audrey!' He called me twice. We jumped up and ran to the pool. I called Roy, who was our gardener, and said, 'Roy, come, we need you!' We got him out of the pool and I did resuscitation, chest and breathing, but I could tell when we got him out of the water he was gone. I told Art Robinson at 9:30 that I could not see myself dragging Albert back to Atlanta. At twelve thirty that afternoon, Albert had a heart attack and was gone.[11]

The logistics of dealing with Albert's death preoccupied her time and thoughts right away.

> Now, I had all of these things to do. I had to go back to Washington, DC, and get clothes because I did not have anything appropriate there. I had to arrange to have Albert's body transported from Jamaica, which is a foreign country, back to the States, to Atlanta, then get to Atlanta myself for Albert's funeral. He was laid to rest in a crypt in Abbey Mausoleum at Westview Cemetery.[12]

While securing his plot, she made arrangements for Dr. Albert E. Manley and Dr. Audrey E. Manley to lay to rest side by side.

> I have often thought of divine interventions in my life. There is no way in the world you can tell me that things happened the way they did without there being a reason. Going back to Spelman, it did not start in January as I first thought it did. It started the year before in March when Johnnetta and I agreed to meet on my birthday. We wanted to be there together. We planned that trip a year earlier. There was no reason to be in Jamaica in March. Albert and I did not go to Jamaica in March; we always went in June, July, or August. But we made the plan the year before, agreeing to go for my birthday. At 9:30 that morning when I said those words to Art, it was more my concern about Albert and his health than what I wanted to do. He was such a wonderful man; but he was President Manley. I knew he would be most unhappy being on campus and he's not the president anymore while I'm doing whatever it is I'm doing. I felt he would not survive that.[13]

She discerned the course of events as a sign that returning to Atlanta and Spelman was destiny. In the least summation, any concern about bringing her husband into an unwanted situation was no longer an issue. It was a difficult pill for her to swallow, but it led her to question what she was supposed to do. The condition of her return came out of her own voice. Albert was the sole basis for her hesitancy. Then, he was gone. The decision to accept the offer to become the president at Spelman College was in the back of her mind, but what was foremost was taking care of her husband.

One chapter in her life had abruptly, unexpectedly, and painfully closed. Another was about to open. It was March 28, 1997.

CHAPTER 12

First Alumna President: A "True Blue" Commitment to Spelman

The work now being done by well-meaning White women will one day be done by well-trained Black women, perhaps one of our own.[1]

—Lucy H. Upton, Spelman College Acting President (1909–1910)

The prophetic vision of Lucy Houghton Upton came to fruition in 1997 when Dr. Audrey Forbes Manley was named the first alumna president of Spelman College. However, a few months prior to the historic announcement, it was necessary to bid a proper farewell to Spelman's fifth president, Dr. Albert Manley. To the gratitude of Dr. Audrey Manley, the tribute was spearheaded by the sitting president of the college at the time, Dr. Johnnetta B. Cole.

Attributing yet another unforeseen course of events to divine order, Dr. Audrey Manley was amazed by the manner in which things unfolded that led her back to Spelman. She elaborated:

> When Albert closed his eyes, it was totally unimaginable. It was so sudden, so unexpected. You have to just picture it, the way the Lord orchestrated things. Albert and I had never vacationed in Jamaica in March. We always went during summer. This time, we agreed to be there for my birthday with Johnetta and Arthur, Johnetta wanting us to spend time there together. And there we were—a Spelman College former president (Albert), the current president (Johnetta), and the future president (even though I was not confirmed at that moment). The three of us were together, playing golf, swimming, drinking tea, and relaxing by the pool. In less than three hours after stating I would not accept the presidency at Spelman and subject Albert to being on campus now that he was retired, he was gone.[2]

Dr. Cole reached out immediately, making final arrangements for Dr. Albert Manley, relieving Dr. Audrey Manley from that responsibility. Dr. Audrey Manley considered the situation to be "the Lord's plan," placing Dr. Cole in the midst of the moments when her husband passed, and having things ordered in a manner that led her to return to Atlanta. She added:

> Dr. Cole told me right away not to worry, that she would take care of everything, and she did. She picked up the phone and called people in Atlanta, Rev. Rates, Joyce Johnson and some of Albert's friends. Dr. Cole reserved Sisters Chapel and handled the details of the service. She took care of Albert, and doing that, she took care of me. The one thing I had to do was arrange the transport of Albert's body from Jamaica to Atlanta. That was a heavy task. But it would have been a very different situation had it happened in Washington, DC, since I was still the acting surgeon general.[3]

News of Dr. Albert Manley's death reverberated rapidly across campus. His homegoing service at Sisters Chapel brought the expected outpouring of Spelman, local and academic communities. Having the service at Sisters Chapel added another dimension to the depth of Dr. Audrey Manley's relationship with the space, resurrecting memories of her first encounter decades earlier when merely walking into the sanctuary took her breath away. On this occasion, she entered with a heavy heart.

She was moved by the number of her Spelman sisters who paid their final respects, the heartfelt, glowing statements made about his character and the things he had done for Spelman, and the gracious manner in which the service was conducted overall, being extremely grateful to Dr. Cole for the latter. Afterward, when several people asked if she was coming back, that, too, touched her deeply.

By the time the institution had ceremoniously remembered Dr. Albert Manley, officials at the college returned their attention quickly to confirming their choice for the future leadership of Spelman. The search committee held an anticipated call meeting. An emergency meeting of the Board of Trustees was held with Dr. Audrey Manley present. The Board wanted to know how she was doing, and if she still felt up to assuming the presidency. They expressed empathy for the sudden manner in which her life had recently changed, realizing that meant she would be settling in the city alone. They wondered if the loss would affect her ability to assume presidential duties on the first day of July. It was stressed that they really needed her in place by that date. She responded honestly, "Yes, I am having a very difficult time right now, but I will be better by the first of

July."[4] Despite her grief, she stood by the commitment, hoping that focusing on Spelman's needs would keep her mind off missing Albert.

Dr. Manley had only three months to tie up professional and personal loose ends and commitments in Washington, DC, before returning to Atlanta by July first. The number one priority was finding someone to take care of her home since there was not enough time to deal with selling it before leaving. A related task was deciding what to take with her to Atlanta—personal items, paintings, and other things that would make the campus house feel more like home without having to make new purchases. It was equally important to go through the exit ritual from her federal appointment.

The relief she felt when Dr. Satcher was confirmed as the new surgeon general was replaced with grief that had to be held in check as she made the transition from leadership on the Washington scene to serving Spelman in Atlanta. With fifteen years in direct healthcare delivery fields as a board certified physician and twenty-one years of professional military service, her professional federal experience included the distinction of being the only person, male or female, to have held all of the top four positions in the US PHS. Each of these was a highlighted point during her retirement celebration. In typical fashion, her special assistant, Captain Steve Moore, spearheaded the organization and execution of her retirement ceremony held at the Uniformed Services University of the Health Sciences (USUHS) in Bethesda. Maryland.

At the academy, she was greeted by a line of uniformed officers who escorted her into the auditorium. The three hundred people who attended to wish her well included a number of individuals whose presence pleasantly surprised her. She was touched by the tokens of appreciation received, especially a table made by her officers which was unlike anything she had ever seen before. At the conclusion of the celebration, a line of Spelman women marched her out, then formed an arch as a symbolic gesture welcoming her back into the Spelman College fold as the institution's leader. She was visibly moved. The ceremony was her final appearance in a federal capacity in the nation's capital.

On July 1, 1997, Dr. Audrey Forbes Manley joined the legacy of leaders who officiated over the academic institution and became the first alumna elected president of Spelman College.[5] She brought a unique perspective to the presidency, having previously experienced the college as a student, alumna, member of the Board of Trustees and First Lady. The new president also possessed a useful set of skills acquired and fine-tuned over decades of service to communities nationally and on local levels. This enhanced her ability to access federal financial, in-kind and personnel resources beneficial to the college in numerous ways.

By the fifth month of her leadership, Dr. Manley had secured full-time professional support for the Office of the President at no cost to the college. Due to her effort and assistance from Mrs. Vivian Malone Jones, a civil rights activist who integrated the University of Alabama and worked at EPA as director of civil rights and urban affairs and director of environmental justice, Dr. Manley was able to bring Ms. Barbara Boone on board in the capacity as her executive assistant.

Ms. Boone joined the president's office in November, 1997, on assignment from the federal government through the Intergovernmental Personnel Act (IPA) Mobility Program.[6] A human resources specialist who was human resource officer over personnel and facility management, and program manager at EPA, Ms. Boone expected to be assigned to support a professor when her interview was scheduled. The date of her interview turned out to be a dreary late fall day with extremely heavy downpours. Locating a place to park was nearly impossible, and by the time she made her way to the President's Office in Rockefeller Hall for the interview, she was wet and winded. Dr. Manley's greeting included an apology for having her come out on such a rainy day, then the two engaged in a conversation, which revealed their compatibility.

Their government ties and understanding of organizational structure confirmed they could work together effectively. In order to support Dr. Manley, Ms. Boone recognized it was necessary to pattern her work schedule according to the president's needs. She discovered it was far from the usual work assignment. Ms. Boone stated: "What I thought was a 9 to 5 turned out to be a 9 to 9, 24/7 and every day overtime…AND! I had to buy my own lunch."[7] Then she added: "But it was worth it. I had the utmost respect for Dr. Audrey Forbes Manley's commitment and devotion to Spelman. I witnessed her tireless work ethic up close and personal." Because they had similar work styles, it was an easy transition with a spirit of professional trust and understanding between them. Ms. Boone further explained, "Even though no specific duties were outlined, I carved out my own duties and responsibilities based on what was needed."[8] With the desired stability in her office, Dr. Audrey Manley continued to assess what was most needed for the college at that point in time.

Many students during this time took to heart the implications of matriculating under the watchful eye of an alumna president. The 1998 graduating class summed up the corporate appreciation of her contributions to her field and to Spelman's legacy in several student yearbook entries. Kandace A. Totten, editor-in-chief of *Reflections* in 1998, and staff writer Natalie H. Veeney wrote a poem titled "Leading The Way" (1998), which included lines that outlined Dr. Audrey Forbes Manley's placement within the legacy of their beloved Spelman:

"Spelman College has continued to demonstrate her legacy of greatness... She is our classmate, she is our President, she is our roommate...She is our best friend, she is our sister. From every angle she is one."[9] In the same edition, President Manley is acknowledged for her role as one of the founders of the yearbook, *Reflections,* in 1955.

The following year, Dr. Manley's formal Presidential inauguration ceremony was held on Saturday, October 31, 1998. On the occasion, she accepted the charge of leadership, concluding with a statement on the

> Institutions thrive only if—only when they honor their connections to the past, indeed, their indebtedness to the past, without being imprisoned, crippled, limited, or blinded by that connectedness. Institutions thrive only if—only when they place their feet deeply in the soil of their past and reach with unencumbered hands into the open space of possibilities.[10]

The ritual inspired the spring graduating class to elaborate on the implications of "True Blue," a descriptive they felt was applicable to their Spelman Sister President. As the first African American woman to serve on the full faculty at the University of Chicago School of Medicine in the Department of Pediatrics and to have a full-time faculty position at Emory University, academic firsts positioned her for the military firsts that followed. *Reflections* staff paid specific tribute to Dr. Audrey Manley for her military career achievements with the theme "Dreaming, daring, Doing...Keeping the Legacy Alive." Editor-in-chief Teresa M. Howell led with the following:

> As we celebrate the inauguration of our first alumna president here at Spelman, we have adopted the theme "True Blue." More than the apparent tie to Spelman's color with the event, "True Blue" is the most appropriate, accurate and simplest way of capturing the spirit of Audrey Forbes Manley, specifically as it relates to her beloved Spelman. The story of this woman and her great accomplishments is one of epic proportions. Dr. Audrey Forbes Manley's life represents a commitment to Spelman's future and a career of many firsts:

Former Acting Surgeon General
Former Deputy Surgeon General
First African American Female Assistant Surgeon General (Rear Admiral)
First African American Female Acting Assistant Secretary for Health
First African American Female Deputy Assistant Secretary for Health
Former Director of the National Health Services Corps
First African American Female Chief Resident at Cook County Children's Hospital
A career of firsts, a commitment to Spelman.

The tribute concludes: "True Blue does not fade. It does not imitate or reflect other colors. It resists impurities. It is authentically and intensely itself."[11]

An early priority for Dr. Manley was taking a walking tour of the campus to view the facilities. Observing where things were, how things were going, what changes had occurred, and which things had not changed, helped her identify matters that were urgent or not so urgent. The two-week process was enlightening. It was clear that core campus buildings needed immediate attention which made the physical plant her first priority. She developed a blueprint for the future in a master plan, which outlined her vision for Spelman's future growth and success. Stand-out points in the plan were renovation and restoration of campus facilities, land acquisition, access to technology and the institutionalized delivery of community service, creation of a student-centered environment, and alumni empowerment. She believed these things were in the best interest of students and the college.

Dr. Manley was pleased that a number of people had remained in key staff positions. She worked closely with the vice president for business and financial affairs, Mr. Robert "Danny" Flanigan, Jr. President Albert Manley brought Danny Flanigan on board in 1970 as assistant to the business manager. "Danny," as he was called by everyone, gradually moved up to the vice president position. She thought that having the lead management person remain a steward of Spelman's finances over decades gave the office perpetuity.

Like most leaders, Dr. Manley had a particular way of working. She assessed what was needed then mapped out a strategy in detail for getting it done. The process was discussed with senior administrative staff. To her, the most important engagement on the front end was with Mr. Robert "Danny" Flanigan. As was her custom, she laid everything out meticulously on a flip chart. Every goal and corresponding task was indicated. Both the items and the chart were retained. With the list on the flip chart completed, she went over each entry thoroughly with Danny. He followed her intensely. When she finished, he asked, "Can I have that?" Not thinking—she usually held on to it for her own point of reference—she replied, "Of course," then shared her candid perspective on the physical condition of the campus. She concluded:

> "You are here every day. When you are sitting in a situation day after day, month after month, year after year, everything tends to appear to be fine. But when you go away and come back, you can see the difference. You notice the changes that have occurred over time.[12]

She began to understand why her recruitment was so vigorous by the board and some faculty members.

Dr. Falconer, a longstanding distinguished professor heading up the science department, had been successful at getting grants and financial support from NIH, National Science Foundation (NSF), and other sources over the years. Much of the equipment needed for study remained on the floor and in the hallways of Tapley Hall due to a lack of space. The urgent need to renovate Tapley was obvious, and there were buildings across the campus that needed updating as well. Dr. Manley was mindful of the fact that Spelman was a small campus, encompassing just under twelve miles with buildings originally concentrated from the center out, not in an expansive, sprawling pattern. Therefore, it was not feasible to execute more than two building projects at a time in order to insure there were sufficient spaces to accommodate student requirements and faculty needs.

Her familiarity with federal departments, procedures, and assistance capabilities increased the likelihood of successful applications for support. She was well regarded across governmental spheres with a track record for getting things done according to schedule, in the manner promised and according to high quality standards. Her expressed hope was "to expediate the agenda with respect for Spelman's long-held traditions that had helped shape its purpose and identity, while at the same time having a regard for positive changes that would move the college forward as it continued to fulfill its mission."[13]

MacVicar and Tapley Halls were targeted first. Historic MacVicar Hall was built in 1901 and housed the college healthcare facilities and Women's Health Program. Named for education superintendent Malcolm MacVicar of the American Baptist Home Mission Society, restoration began the first of October in 1998.[14] The building was totally renovated with the addition of new construction of an attached 17,000 square-foot, two-story infirmary. All aspects of the design and materials matched that of the historic structure. The original hardwood floors were retained. Renovation and construction costs were covered by a grant from the National Institute of Health, OMH. The project was completed in 2000.

To launch construction of a facility to accommodate the increased demand for science space, Dr. Manley held a ribbon cutting ceremony at the site of the future Science Center. During the construction ceremony, a time capsule was donated to be opened in 25 years after the completion of the structure. In 2001 The Albro-Falconer-Manley Science Center was completed. A state-of-the-art complex designed as an interdisciplinary learning and research center for the natural sciences, mathematics, and computer science, the center immediately became a hub for activities conducive to intellectual exchange, scientific creativity, and innovative uses of technology. The center also enhanced the ability of the college to attract and prepare students in these disciplines. Significant financial support had begun under the administration of President Johnetta B. Cole. Under Dr. Manley, funds were now provided by the NSF, the NIH, and the David and Lucile Packard Foundation.

The center was named in honor of contributions to the college of biology Professor Dr. Helen T. Albro, associate provost and Professor Dr. Etta Z. Falconer, and President Dr. Audrey Forbes Manley.

Tapley Hall (1925), dedicated to Spelman's third president, Lucy Hale Tapley (1857–1932) was also refurbished as part of the project By the time construction initiated, Spelman had the reputation for being the number two school in the country for placing African American students in medical school, according to the Association of Medical Colleges (2000). With attention afforded the sciences, the numbers continued to grow. Programs grew to where there were, at one count, 450 Spelman graduates in medicine, pharmacology, and health careers, and 150 PhDs in mathematics.

The remaining buildings on the president's priority list were Packard Hall (built c. 1887) and Sisters Chapel (constructed in 1927). Packard and Sisters Chapel were two campus structures that dated back to founders Ms. Sofia B. Packard (1824–1891) and Ms. Harriet E. Giles (1828–1909). Packard Hall was one of the oldest buildings on campus, one of the original buildings located on Spelman's historic quadrangle, and was identified as an endangered structure in 1988 by the National Park Service. Dr. Manley called attention to the significance of the history and function of Packard at Spelman, as she had done with previous initiatives, to secure support for its renovation. In 2001, the US Department of Interior, Historic Preservation Initiative for Historic Black Colleges and Universities administered by the National Park Service, provided over $900,000 in a matching grant for the extensive restoration of Packard's exterior, reconfiguration from a dormitory to administrative offices and the addition of stair wings on its interior.

When Danny Flanigan asked, "Are we going to get a dormitory?" referring to the work that would soon begin on Packard, Dr. Manley informed him that the new Packard Hall would function as part of the administrative structure. This was music to his ears since Danny's operations were spread out at various locations around campus. She recognized the building had out-lived its original function as a dormitory, that even post-renovation, it would not offer enough bedspace for Spelman's current housing needs. The new Packard Hall was to serve as a centralized hub for student services and maintain the character and form of the original structure.[15]

Vice President for Student Affairs and Dean of Students Dr. Zenobia Lawrence Hikes (1955–2008) enlightened students about the status of the former dormitory during the final town hall meeting for the 2000–2001 academic year of the Spelman Student Government Association (SSGA). At the April 10, 2001 meeting, Dean Hikes shared general information regarding the building to students, assuring them that "all Freshwomen would be guaranteed housing during the 2001–2002 school year, despite the upcoming renovation of Packard Hall."[16]

With the funding for the Packard Hall project sufficiently underway, President Manley directed attention to Sisters Chapel. Dedicated in 1927, Sisters Chapel was one of the most important buildings on campus. Sisters Chapel was named for its primary donors, sisters Mrs. Laura Spelman Rockefeller (1839–1915), and Lucy Maria Spelman (1837–1920), the mother and aunt of major Spelman College benefactor John D. Rockefeller, Jr. (1884–1960). The 1,200-seat-capacity facility from its inception served as the spiritual center of Spelman College, and became an important focal point of college life.

Its history included being the site of the inauguration of the much-loved annual Spelman–Morehouse Christmas Carol Concert that it has hosted annually since 1927. Sisters Chapel took the international stage in 1968 when thousands of mourners from around the world filed into the building to show final respects to Dr. Martin Luther King, Jr. lying in state as organist, Dr. Joyce Finch Johnson, contributed to the ambience by playing quiet, reflective spirituals.

Dr. Manley considered Sisters Chapel the greatest challenge on the restoration list, while assuring the Board of Trustees there was nothing to worry about because alumnae would participate. That was a key component of her planned approach, to engage her sister alumnae. Sisters Chapel was near and dear to her heart. She knew her Spelman sisters felt the same way, and envisioned its renovation would be a project driven and achieved largely by them. In addition to wanting to see Sisters Chapel refurbished, air conditioning and restrooms were among the specifics needed. She admitted,

> It never dawned on me before that the absence of bathrooms could be an issue. I suppose when you have young people, it's not a problem. But now we have alumnae returning often with it being commonly used, and they are seventy, eighty plus years. We are now open to increased public attendance on the campus as well.[17]

Assisted by the Office of Alumnae Affairs, an alumnae group was formed to help with fundraising, generating appropriate meetings and interacting in various ways with chapters nationwide.

During the process, it came to Dr. Manley's attention that Spelman had received an offer for a challenge grant in the past to contribute to the renovation of Sisters Chapel from a local organization that wanted to remain anonymous. They had offered the gift over a period of three or four years without receiving a response. It was emphasized that if the organization did not hear something soon, they would forget about it. Dr. Manley quickly arranged a meeting with the prospective donors and explained that with two building projects well underway—Packard Hall and the science center—it was ill-advised for Spelman to take on more than that number at a time. However, she assured them that Sisters Chapel would be next. She shared the layout of the school's action plan with them, which indicated that Sisters Chapel was the subsequent target of restoration and refurbishing on the part of the college. Expressing satisfaction with the plan, they agreed to wait. In due time, the challenge grant and contributions from alumnae made it possible to move forward with an architectural design and plan for Sisters Chapel.

In addition to upgrading the physical condition of Sisters Chapel, the president believed it was time to preserve the history of the iconic structure as well. To her, no one was better equipped for the assignment than the college minister, Rev. Norman Rates. Dr. Manley presented the idea to Rev. Rates to write a history of Sisters Chapel, acknowledging his breadth of knowledge of the building's past, his longevity of service as a professor of religion and minister, and his commitment to the faith-based mission of the college. Rev. Rates began working on the book after his retirement. *May Thy Dear Walls Remain: Memoirs of a College Minister at Sisters Chapel at Spelman College* was published in 2010.[18] Dr. Manley praised the publication as "an excellent book that, in telling the story, captured the thoughts and feelings students and alumnae have for Sisters Chapel."[19]

Attending to the college infrastructure and legacy was driven by a greater awareness of the need to serve students comprehensively, a goal Dr. Manley understood included identifying qualified administrative leadership as well as outstanding faculty. In 2001, the president hired Rev. Lisa D. Rhodes to succeed Rev. Rates as Dean of Sisters Chapel. Rev. Rhodes had studied psychology at Wheeling College and completed master's requirements in clinical social work at the University of Maryland before receiving a master of divinity degree from the Candler School of Theology at Emory University and doctorate of Ministry from Union Theological Seminary, Presbyterian School for Christian Education. Formerly an assistant pastor at Ebenezer Baptist Church in Atlanta, she served as Director of the Sisters Center for WISDOM (Women in Spiritual Discernment of Ministry), a Center of Distinction she envisioned and led at the college. Rev. Rhodes restored an emphasis on mentoring, counseling, and advising at Spelman, addressing the personal needs of hundreds of students. She served as a contextual education supervisor for seminary students at several theological intuitions in the Atlanta area.

When the need arose to fill the dean of students position, the president looked within the existing ranks of faculty and professional staff. Dr. Manley offered the opportunity to Dr. Cynthia Neal Spence, a Spelman alumna with advanced training in Criminal Justice at Rutgers University. Dr. Spence joined the Department of Sociology and Anthropology in 1981, later assuming additional duties as Assistant Dean for Freshman Studies and later as Associate Dean. She shared Dr. Manley's commitment to addressing the needs of students on a one-on-one basis as well as through corporate engagement, and encouraging them to seek effective means to merging educational goals, social interests, and community engagement.

Dr. Pauline E. Drake served as interim provost while the search to fill that post was underway. Dr. Drake was valedictorian of her Spelman graduating class, and completed studies and attended Bowling Green State University before receiving the PhD from the University of Pittsburgh. She began working at Spelman in 1974 in the Department of Education. The following year she was named Director of The Institute for Teaching and Learning, and became head of the Continuing Education Program when it was initiated in the early 1980s. Dr. Drake led the expansion of the Continuing Education Program from being the provider of non-credit courses for community residents to being a unit that included Elderhostel—an international program for mature adults, summer institutes for college faculty, summer and after-school programs for youth, non-credit training for employees of various organizations, and the program for mature women beginning or returning to college to earn a bachelor's degree. The program was ultimately named the Pauline E. Drake Scholars (PEDS) Program.[20]

Exploring means to achieving physical expansion was another issue Dr. Manley cared about. She was encouraged in the early days of her administration by Mrs. Carolyn "Marge" Dunbar Yancey (1921–2010). Mrs. Yancey had been a Trustee of the college for twenty-five years when she showed up unannounced at the Office of the President two weeks after Dr. Manley arrived. In addition to being motivated to push for possible land growth as a board member, Mrs. Yancey was interested because her daughter, Dr. Carolyn Lois Yancey, had attended Spelman (C72). Once Dr. Manley approved her entry, Mrs. Yancey wasted no time explaining why she was there: "I don't have much time. I don't know how much longer I'm going to be living. So, I just have one thing to say to you, Dr. Manley. You have got to get some land for Spelman."[21] That was the gist of what she had to say. Dr. Manley recalled, "It was as if a light bulb went off, like a hit over the head. I knew she was right. We were all (the AUC schools) hemmed in by public housing. It was especially the case with Spelman."[22]

Spelman was surrounded by three public housing properties that were, for the most part, deteriorating. They were prospects worth consideration for possible land acquisition. John Hope Homes, built in 1940 on Greensferry Avenue was next to pre-existing University Homes, bounded in part by Spelman Street and Spelman Lane. The John Hope Homes project was demolished in 2000 and redeveloped by H.J. Russell and Company as the Villages at Castleberry Hill, an Atlanta Housing-sponsored mixed-income, mixed-finance community with modern features. This removed John Hope Homes from consideration.

University Homes was the first federally funded public housing for African Americans in the US. Built in 1938 on a site known at the time as Beaver Slide, University Homes mostly bordered Clark Atlanta University. Being the farthest public housing from the college, Dr. Manley chose to target something closer to the Gates of Spelman, namely Harris Homes. Harris Homes was constructed in 1956 on Ashby Street (in 2001 the city changed the name to Joseph E. Lowery Boulevard). Determined to put forth the strongest effort possible to secure nearby land, Dr. Manley felt it was not an action Spelman should attempt alone. She found an immediate ally in Morehouse College President Dr. Walter E. Massey. They had a good professional working relationship, shared similar ideas about collegial matters, and agreed that spatial growth was an ideal pursuit. She then solicited the involvement of Morehouse School of Medicine President Louis W. Sullivan, another academic leader with whom she had a positive and productive collaborative work history. The three presidents met and strategized about the best approach to take to convince the Atlanta Housing Authority (AHA) that their plan would ultimately be in the public good.

Dr. Manley was the catalyst for conceiving a means to collectively facilitate land acquisition. The result was the establishment of College Partners, Incorporated (CPI) which became official on April 20, 2000. CPI's mission was to provide financial support for the acquisition of real estate in areas surrounding Spelman College, Morehouse College, and Morehouse School of Medicine.[23] Her vision was to get the AHA to sell some of that land that was a part of public housing closest to their campuses. This would make for possible expansion or, at least, serve as a buffer. She had assisted other communities in the past with making it happen, Harvard University in Connecticut being one example. It was time to work toward the same for institutions in the AUC. She regretted it took the schools so long and that AHA was not as receptive to the idea as the presidents had hoped.

The AHA made the case that they could not legally sell any part of Harris Homes to CPI outright, but were willing to accommodate their request if it was a land swap. CPI decided to purchase land bordering one side of Morehouse College in order to participate in an exchange with the AHA property at the public housing site. They were, eventually, successful at acquiring a portion of land at the Harris Homes location. Her idea worked, even though the project itself was not fully finalized until after she retired. She did witness the United States Department of Housing and Urban Development (HUD) Authority representative signing the authorization paperwork for the purchase of the land. This gave her a sense of relief knowing the college would have a little more than six acres of buffer zone.

Improvement was needed on the technology front as well, and was another priority item in her master plan. When Dr. Manley took the helm of Spelman, an Atlanta University Center-wide system was under discussion which would allow a student attending any of the AUC colleges to cross register for classes at any of the center schools. However, the institutions disagreed on which system to use. The gridlock had lasted two years with no sign of resolution. Meanwhile, registration remained problematic too often for students and faculty.

She concluded, "Enough is enough. A common system is fine if operational. But I came here to take care of Spelman. Spelman will move forward and we will have our own system."[24] Dr. Manley made her position clear that it was detrimental to students to be denied access to an effective registration process, not in the best interest of faculty to be without accurate registration rolls in a timely and efficient manner, and was potentially problematic for the Office of Registration with the decision of a unified system being in limbo. Getting the proper technology system in place meant hiring a professional who knew how to do it. A new position was created, vice president for information technology. In 2001, the Division of Media and Information Technology was established. It meant that, once every dormitory and classroom was online and operative, then the decision would be made about who Spelman would cross connect with. She was convinced it saved the college.

Recruiting talented professors and retaining excellent faculty were central to her goal for advancing a student-centered environment that would best prepare graduates for career success. In her opinion, achieving this two-pronged goal was more likely if Spelman improved salaries. She stated:

> It was an easy sell to the board—that if we did not pay good people what they deserve they would go someplace else. The board was generous. Before I could make a real pitch, they set aside a million dollars to upgrade faculty salaries. Improving faculty salaries, the board did it.[25]

Accomplished professionals were brought in as faculty or in guest and other capacities during her tenure "to engage, enlighten and inspire students to commit to excellence and service." In 2000, Dr. Gloria Wade Gayles returned to Spelman with a distinguished record as the author of four books, numerous articles in academic journals and editor of two anthologies. She had been a DuBois Fellow at Harvard University, CASE Professor of Teaching Excellence for the State of Georgia, recipient of an Honorary Doctor of Humane Letters from Meadville-Lombard Theological School of the University of Chicago, Eminent Scholar's Chair at Dillard University, and recipient of the Emory University Medal.[26] At Spelman, she was named Eminent Scholar's Chair in Independent Scholarship and Service Learning under the Faculty-In-Residence Program within the Division of Liberal Arts and Education.[27]

Dr. Gayles founded The Spelman Independent Scholars Program (SIS), the first and only oral history project at an undergraduate institution in the nation conducting extensive interviews with African American women elders in the South aged from sixty-five to 103 to capture firsthand accounts of lives in the previous century.[28] The following year, she became founding director of RESONANCE, a student choral performance group whose original scripts advance African American cultural expression and history.

The college provided a number of additional supportive entities for its students. In 2000 the Women in Excellence Leadership Series (WEL) was established. This program was designed as a seven-week intensive study course for juniors and seniors to provide advanced-level training in preparation for leadership roles in the global community.

The first William and Camille Cosby Endowed Professorship, referred to as the Cosby Chair, was awarded in the fine arts in 2001 to film and video artist Dr. Ayoka Chenzira.[29] A film graduate of New York University (BFA), Columbia University Teachers College in education (MA), and Georgia Institute of Technology in digital media (PhD), Dr. Chenzira was considered the first African American female animator and a pioneer in Black Independent cinema and transmedia storytelling. Directors Guild of America member and founding director of the award-winning Digital Moving Image Salon (DMIS). In addition, she Dr. Chenzia also served as co-director of Oral Narratives and Digital Technology, a joint venture between Spelman College and the Durham Institute of Technology.

The 2002 endowed professorship in the fine arts was awarded to Spelman alumna Bernice Johnson Reagon (Class of 1970 [C'70]). The celebrated singer, song leader, civil rights activist, and cultural historian was founder-director of the a cappella group the Harambe Singers (1968–1970) and the celebrated group Sweet Honey in the Rock (1970–2004). Among her numerous honors are a George F. Peabody Award as principal scholar, conceptual producer, and host of the Smithsonian Folkways and National Public Radio series *Wade in the Water: African American Sacred Music Traditions*. Bernice Reagon was the recipient of a Charles E. Frankel Prize, Presidential Medal for outstanding contributions to public understanding of the humanities, MacArthur Fellows Program award, and the Martin Luther King, Jr. Center for Nonviolent Social Change Trumpet of Conscience Award, among others.

That same year, cultural anthropologist and documentary filmmaker Dr. Sheila S. Walker was named endowed Professor in the Humanities. Holding degrees from Bryn Mawr College (BA) and the University of Chicago (PhD), Dr. Walker was previously the Annabel Iron Worsham Centennial Chair in the College of Liberal Arts and Director of the Center for African and African American Studies at the University of Texas at Austin. Her knowledge of African Diaspora global culture formed the bases of her lectures, programs, documentary films, and book,

Conocimiento desde adentro: Los afro-sudamericanos hablan de sus pueblos y sus hisorias/Conhecimento desde dentro: Os afro-sul-americanos falam de seus povos e suas historias (Knowledge from the Inside: Afro-South Americans Speak of their People and their Histories), published in Spanish and Portuguese.

There were several high-profile events that occurred on campus under Dr. Manley's oversight, particularly in 2001. The college marked its eighth year of participation in the Corporate Partners Conference held March 22 and 23, with the theme "Investing in the Top Tier." Spelman hosted a record- breaking number of attendees to the conference, including over fifty-five liaisons representing twenty-five Fortune 500 companies joined by fifty faculty, students, and staff. The conference emphasized the critical need for continued and expanded support from the corporate sector.

In May, President Manley welcomed intellectuals from around the world to campus when the twenty-fifth Annual Conference of the International Association of Philosophy and Literature (IAPL) was held at the college. Spelman became the first historically Black college to host the organization's world-renowned event that was initiated on the campus of Harvard University. More than 300 national and international scholars recognized for their interdisciplinary expertise in the arts, humanities, and social sciences attended. Conference co-coordinators were Spelman faculty members Dr. Beverly Guy-Sheftall, Director of the Women's Center and the Dr. Anna Julia Cooper Professor of Women's Studies, and Dr. Roy Martinez, Chair of the Department of Philosophy and Religion.

Presiding over the college's 100th Commencement ceremony awarding baccalaureate degrees was significant to Dr. Manley for a number of reasons. In addition to the 100 years milestone, a record 515 students received degrees, including the first Asian graduate, Nao Ayabe from Tokyo, Japan. Perhaps due to her Washington, DC ties, President Manley was aware of preparations underway for the sixteenth National Pearl Harbor Remembrance Day; recalled the dramatic impact of the attack on corporate and personal levels; and, considered having a Japanese student complete undergraduate study during her administration a sign of healing and reconciliation.

Throughout Dr. Manley's administration, Spelman remained academically strong and culturally and socially relevant. On February 10, 1998, the Epsilon Chapter of Phi Beta Kappa was installed at Spelman by Dr. David Levering Lewis, Martin Luther King, Jr. University Professor of History at Rutgers University. During the installation of Phi Beta Kappa, the oldest academic honor society in the US and the most prestigious, Dr. Lewis remarked,

> I should like to believe that Phi Beta Kappa's coming to Spelman is fatefully symbolic and represents a milestone in the progress of the life of the mind and of the 'love of learning' (Phi Beta Kappa's motto, indeed) among that half of humanity to whom the nation must turn increasingly for the mediation and attenuation of that patriarchal, racist, sexist, and aggressive past that it so urgently needs to escape.[30]

The chapter held its first initiation ceremony on April 28, 1998 to induct its first group of forty-four undergraduate members.

On February 20, 1998, The National Council of Negro Women, Inc. (NCNW) unveiled its recently chartered chapter at Spelman, making it only the second section in the nation founded on a college campus to improve political, social, and economic conditions of all women by increasing their involvement in issues on local and national levels. Spelman alumna Dr. Jane E. Smith (C'68) took over as president and chief operating officer of NCNW that year following the retirement of Dr. Dorothy L. Height, who had led the organization since 1957.

Further, in 1998, President Manley welcomed the Enhancing Diversity in Graduate Education (EDGE) program to Spelman in its inaugural year. A national program developed to prepare and strengthen the ability of female students to successfully complete graduate programs in the mathematical sciences, EDGE was established by Dr. Sylvia Trimble Bozeman, who served as chair of the Department of Mathematics at Spelman from 1982 to 1993, and Dr. Rhonda Hughes at Bryn Mawr College in Pennsylvania. Dr. Bozeman and Dr. Hughes organized the Spelman-Bryn Mawr Summer Mathematics Program for female undergraduate students from 1992 to 1994. The EDGE program brought in senior graduates and panelists and formed study groups so that participants could learn how to give and receive information critical to graduate school survival.

Dr. Manley had many celebratory occasions to share with her Spelman family in 1999 as well. That year, Spelman was recognized by the Association of Medical Colleges as the number two institution in the US for placing African American students in medical school, and the college also celebrated two senior class recipients of Fulbright Post-Baccalaureate Fellowships for research study abroad. Recognition of the college's academic and cultural success continued to be noted in a number of prominent publications in 1999. *U.S. News & World Report* ranked Spelman the number one liberal arts college for women, and number five among America's best buys for college. *Money Magazine* also highlighted Spelman as the top regional liberal arts college and as a top HBCU in several studies including their annual survey. *Black Enterprise* magazine acknowledged Spelman's number one position for having the best environment for Black collegians, and was recognized as the number two institution on the fifth annual list of Top Ten Activist Schools in the nation by *Mother Jones* magazine.

Supported by the president, the college Chapter of Habitat for Humanity completed its first year of operation in 1999 with more than 125 students, faculty, and staff actively participating in its activities. In addition, the college became a provisional member of the National Collegiate Athletic Association (NCAA) Division II in basketball, volleyball, cross-country, tennis, and track and field.

Under President Manley in 2001, a historic partnership agreement was signed between Spelman College and the University of Delaware. The partnership was designed to enrich curricular and cultural offerings, particularly in the arts, at both institutions. Such an arrangement was among the stipulations of a gift to the University of Delaware by Mr. Paul Raymond Jones (1928–2010), an Atlanta-based business man and art collector who had a long relationship with Spelman College. Paul R. Jones was a strong advocate for Spelman as the initial collaborating HBCU. Jones believed,

> Dr. Manley understood the nuances of such a collaboration and how it can be beneficial to the students, faculty, and college. There are people on faculty that I have interacted with over many years who I think will do what is in the best interest of the college to make it successful.[31]

Faculty and student exchanges, shared distance learning, and teleconferencing with the internet Mr. Jones collection made accessible to Spelman faculty and students via the internet, and opportunities for training in art conservation were some of the main areas Dr. Manley believed would be beneficial.

The partnership got off to a good and official start. Spelman's Chair of the Board of Trustees Dr. June Gary Hopps, President Manley, and University of Delaware President David P. Roselle signed the agreement before a full house during the opening reception of "Through These Eyes: The Photographs of P. H. Polk" on view at the Spelman Museum of Fine Art. The exhibition was organized and originated at Delaware, and was loaned to Spelman with its accompanying publication at no expense to the college. It was the first act of the partnership. In addition, faculty and student exchanges were discussed along with the probability of faculty and student summer institutes.

During her fifth year, The Lilly Foundation, Inc. awarded Spelman a $2 million grant to establish the Sisters Center for WISDOM, the multidimensional, interfaith student-centered leadership development program. The center would officially open its doors after Dr. Manley's retirement in 2003.

Dr. Manley announced her retirement at a college convocation ceremony before a full capacity audience of students, faculty, staff, alumnae, and other members of the Atlanta University Center. She stated:

> When I accepted this position of honor, I identified a number of goals for a five-year tenure that I believed would enhance our distinctive legacy of excellence and service. I have achieved those goals, and it is now my desire to rejoin the ranks of alumnae who serve the college in innumerable ways away from the Gates of Spelman.[32]

The degree to which Dr. Manley met her expressed goals was reiterated in comments by board chair Dr. Hopps, who first applauded President Manley for recruiting the largest class in Spelman's history, then continued:

> Dr. Manley is a futuristic thinker who established an unprecedented partnership with the neighborhood, organizations and other colleges affected by the community. After five years, Spelman enjoyed a balanced budget and increased asset growth of more than $30 million. Dr. Manley has been an effective fundraiser, generating more than $60 million during the past four years. Under her watchful eye, the endowment grew by more than $63 million and physical plant growth by more than $50 million in just four years. The college renovated several buildings, strengthened its infrastructure, and completed fundraising for the 30.8 million Science Complex and raised $2.1 million for the restoration of Sisters Chapel.[33]

The college received a $365,000 grant from The Office of Women's Health at the NIH of The HHS to support The Spelman College Health and Wellness Initiative. Spearheaded by Dr. Manley, the initiative was designed to take a holistic approach that would integrate physical, mental, and spiritual health issues with race-, gender-, and culture-specific tools to reshape the behaviors and attitudes of young African American women (age: eighteen to twenty-two). Plans were implemented to engage students in the initiative effective the upcoming fall.

Dr. Hopps concluded:

> Dr. Manley has done an outstanding job for our students, this community, and this institution. She has taken Spelman to greater heights building on the legacy of seven earlier great presidents. We are sad to see her go, but we understand her wish to retire from active duty. Dr. Manley promises to be around when Spelman needs her, and we can't ask more than that.[34]

External expressions of appreciation came from various sources over the final months of her tenure at the helm of Spelman. During an internationally televised, star-studded special that aired on February 23, 2002, Dr. Audrey Forbes Manley received the Tower of Power Award at the Tenth Annual Trumpet Awards. Presented by Turner Broadcasting System, Inc., the Trumpet Awards were dedicated to honoring accomplished African Americans in such diverse areas as the arts, medicine, government, law, entertainment and science "who succeeded with excellence despite immense odds." Founder Mrs. Xernona Clayton Brady went on to state the recipients "rose above personal achievement to help others along the way."[35] Dr. Manley was honored for her achievements in medicine, with an emphasis on "her enormous contributions to our society and the world which have enriched the lives of others."[36]

The giving of her time and professional talent was noted again by the Turner Broadcasting System, Inc. one month later on May 22, 2002 when President Manley was named one of seventeen individuals in the Atlanta Metropolitan community who, according to the network's selection panel, "volunteered their time and efforts to make a difference in other people's lives." As the Super 17 Award Winner in Education, Dr. Manley was "heralded for encouraging and equipping Spelman students to participate in a number of community service projects, and for her key role in the revitalization of the College's neighboring West End area."[37] As part of the award, Turner Broadcasting produced a story segment on Dr. Manley, which was featured on InterAct Atlanta, the station's public affairs program.

At the 118th commencement of Morehouse College on May 19, President Dr. Walter E. Massey presented Dr. Manley with the Honorary Doctorate of Humane Letters. It marked the first time that a Spelman alumna was bestowed the honor. Later, she made a humorous comment referring to herself as a "Morehouse man." An additional layer of irony and humor derived from the fact of her having attended chemistry classes as the only female student at Morehouse College in the 1950s.

"In The House With Audrey Manley" was a cover story article in the May 2002 issue of *Atlanta GOODlife* magazine. The journal highlighted Reynolds Cottage, the presidential residence at Spelman College, covering the history of the Cottage, its antique furnishings, and its former residents, along with elements of Dr. Manley's unique personal and professional experiences related to the four-level, thirty-two-room Victorian house.

Not to be outdone in showing appreciation for her legacy as an accomplished medical professional, national leader and alumna who proudly stated "If I were to bleed, you would see that my blood is True Blue," the National Alumnae Association of Spelman College (NAASC) initiated the Blue Diamond Awards in her honor. The gala event was held during Founders Week on April 6, 2002, hosted by couples Julius "Dr. J" Irving and Turquoise Irving, and Samuel L. Jackson and alumna Latanya Richardson Jackson (C'74).

That same season on June 19, Atlanta and Decatur Chapters of the NAASC unveiled a bronze plaque on campus commemorating Dr. Manley's 45 years of service to Spelman. The 24″ × 32″ plaque featured a portrait of Dr. Manley with a descriptive citation of her degrees, levels of associations with the college culminating with her term as alumna president, and information about alumnae funding.[38]

Eloise Abernathy Alexis (C'86), director of alumnae affairs during the time when Dr. Manley was at the helm of the college, offered her impressions of the president, indicating:

> I was in awe daily watching Dr. Manley as president couple her administrative savvy with her uncompromised belief in the mission of Spelman. In a powerfully unassuming manner, she wielded unprecedented change and growth in the infrastructure of the College in just five years. Under her watch, our reality has come into alignment with our reputation for excellence.[39]

Dr. Manley exited the office in Rockefeller Hall as President of the college for the last time, departed Reynolds Cottage as her campus home on a second occasion and exited through the Spelman Gate closing one life phase while embarking on another. On her way to Atlanta's airport, she instructed the driver to make one stop—to Abbey Mausoleum in Westview Cemetery where Albert's remains were entombed. She made a final visit to say good-bye to her husband before continuing to Hartsfield-Jackson Airport where she made her scheduled flight and left Atlanta. It was the summer of 2002.

Epilogue

Final Return to Washington, DC

Retiring from the presidency at Spelman College did not usher her into a life of leisure and relaxation right away. Less than two months after leaving Atlanta, she traveled to Newark, Delaware, on August 22, 2002, to receive the honorary doctor of science degree from the University of Delaware. The ceremony occurred during the New Student Convocation, where her impressive career example inspired members of the Class of 2006. She returned to Washington to continue addressing tasks that had to be undertaken and important personal life decisions that had to be made.

At the top of her to-do list was deciding how to clear out the four-story home she once shared with her late husband. It was a daunting endeavor, with the greatest challenge being dealing with Dr. Albert Manley's office on the top floor. He had not thrown anything away. The room was filled with collections of papers and books amassed over his long academic career, including cancelled checks dating back to 1946. The situation was compounded by her own numerous personal items. It took her five years to clear the study.

With that mammoth job behind her, it was necessary to find a new home. She had no desire to remain in Washington especially because of the winters. The agreed-upon plan was for her and her sister to identify a city where they could live closer to one another. With that intent, Dr. Manley conversed with her sister Barbara in Chicago to determine the best place for them to "retire" together. They narrowed their focus to places in the state of Florida, Hilton Head in South Carolina, and Las Vegas, Nevada. They chose Las Vegas based on the weather, entertainment options, affordable real estate, and no state taxes.

Once settled in her new home, Dr. Manley was befriended by Mrs. Kimberly Bailey-Tureaud and her family. A native of Las Vegas and a Spelman alumna, Mrs. Tureaud and her husband Charles were prominent local figures in media, cultural affairs, and community activism. As owners of Culturally Diverse

Advertising (CDA), LLC, they published the *Las Vegas Black Image*. Kimberly Tureaud was the daughter of dancer Anna Bailey and Mr. William H. "Bob" Bailey, a Morehouse graduate who was the first African American television personality in Las Vegas. He was an entrepreneur and civil rights pioneer. Excited to have Dr. Manley in the city and community where she was born and lived, Mrs. Tureaud made herself available to visit and assist Dr. Manley whenever and however she needed her.

Their relationship was bound by Spelman connections and true friendship. Personal interest and professional insight on Kimberly Tureaud's part culminated in her securing permission to conduct an interview of Dr. Manley in her Las Vegas home. The interview offered a candid overview of Dr. Manley's career in healthcare, emphasizing topics related to infant mortality, sickle cell disease, the Genetic Diseases Act, and funding African American students to study medicine. Dr. Manley also mentioned her greatest sources of inspiration.[1]

Dr. Manley was honored in 2020 when the Board of the EDGE Foundation established the Manley-McPherson Presidential Fund for EDGE. The fund was named for Dr. Manley and Dr. Mary Patterson McPherson who were presidents of Spelman and Bryn Mawr Colleges when the EDGE Summer Program was initiated at the two institutions in 1998. Alumnae of the respective colleges they came to lead, Dr. Manley and Dr. McPherson "welcomed the program to their campuses, created an academic environment where such faculty initiatives were nurtured and valued, and supported the program as it grew and expanded. They shepherded their institutions to greatness and committed themselves to values embraced by the mission of The EDGE Foundation."[2]

In retirement, Dr. Audre Forbes Manley continued to insist that none of the credit for her achievements and successes were her own. She insisted that through faith and by grace, "God had his hand on her"; that life's opportunities were presented "right in front of her"; and that her steps were ordered. Nevertheless, the impact she had on subsequent generations of doctors, scientists, health administrators, and others directly and indirectly bears witness to an accomplished life and legacy.

Over the course of her career, Dr. Audrey Forbes Manley managed to be all things Spelman—student, alumna, board member, benefactor, first lady, and president. Her impact on younger fellow alumnae cannot be denied, and is, perhaps, best summarized in the poetic voice of Amena J. Brown (C'02) in "Inaugural Poem: A Legacy Continued":

When the voice of mediocrity spoke, we listened.
When the voice of mistakes past had the last
Word, we Harkened and turned our ear
Our heart
Collectively
Because it was easy and comfortable
Respectively.
Reflectively, I stand at an impasse
Connecting to future to present to past.
Why, I ask, have I come for such a time as this?
A time for cheeks to be kissed and shoulders caressed,
Because when we look to our president, we see our best.
We see our struggles, we see our pain
Our heartache, our triumph, our gain
In the one who has been selected
Who in the mirror of Spelman legacy is reflected.
When the voice of excellence speaks, we listen.
When the voice of futures prominent has
The first say, we
Heed and incline ourselves
Our souls, our minds, our bodies,
Our commitment and faith
Our support and our strength
As we lift the arms of the one who has been bestowed upon us.
The one who demanded she would not allow anyone
To suppress her into merely being someone,
And the great thing is that she is one
Of us.
Audrey Forbes Manley is not just a name,
But a legacy;
A story to be passed,
To be told by our
Spelman mothers to our
Spelman daughters and our
Spelman sisters,
Directly.
Reflectively, I stand at an impasse

Connecting to future to present to past,
Why, you ask, has she come for such a time as this?
A time for negativity and disunity to be dismissed.
A time for cheeks to be kissed and shoulders caressed,
Because we have gained a president who brings forth, not only her own
But our best.[3]

NOTES

Chapter 1

1. Dr. Audrey Forbes Manley July 8, 2020 phone interview with the author.
2. Reportedly, tens of millions of people listened to President Roosevelt's nineteenth "fireside chat" announcing the US declaration of war, including many African Americans in small and rural areas who gathered in hearing range of the limited radios that were accessible.
3. The East St. Louis Riot of 1917 was a series of outbreaks of labor- and race-related violence by White Americans stemming from the employment of 470 African Americans to replace White workers who had gone on strike against the Aluminum Ore Company. Triggered by a rumor on July 1, the next day, riots—mostly drive-by-shootings, beatings and arson—lasted for nearly a week, leaving nine Whites and hundreds of African Americans dead and property damage estimated at $400,000. More than 6,000 African American citizens fled the city fearing for their lives.

Chapter 2

1. Lemann, who was a contributing editor to *The Atlantic*, enjoyed positive receptivity of his book, which was considered a groundbreaking history of the migration of African Americans from the rural South to the urban North when released in 1991. The publication was popular among academics, readers of American history topics related to the civil rights movement, and general print readers.
2. The Southside Community Art Center dates back to the late 1930s when members of the Chicago-based African American artist group, Arts Craft Guild, were on the forefront of its development. Guild members included Dr. Margaret Taylor-Burroughs, Eldzier Cortor, Bernard Goss, Charles White, William Carter, Joseph Kersey, and Archibald Motley.
3. Although Wendell Phillips is the oldest Black high school in Chicago, it is opened as a predominately White school on September 4, 1904. Phillips had replaced South Division High School, which had been located at 26th and Wabash since 1875. Phillips served the wealthy children in the community and the few African American children of their servants.
4. Since 2005, the DuSable High School campus has served as the site of two smaller institutions: the Bronzeville Scholastic Institute and the Daniel Hale Williams Preparatory School of Medicine. The structure was designated a Chicago historic landmark in 2015.
5. Manley's July 8, 2020 interview.
6. According to the American Medical Association, "schizophrenia is the most chronic and disabling of the major mental illnesses. It can leave the sufferer frightened and withdrawn, and is a lifelong disease that cannot be cured but can be controlled with proper treatment."
7. Dr. Audrey Forbes Manley's phone interview with the author, on February 9, 2020.

Chapter 3

1. *Fortune* magazine published the article featuring "Sweet Auburn" in 1956. *The Atlanta Journal-Constitution's* comments refer to the *Fortune* article when concurring in "Life with Gracie: Preserving Sweet Auburn One Block at a Time" in the 2017 by columnist Gracie Bond Staples.
2. Albert E. Manley. *A Legacy Continues: The Manley Years at Spelman College, 1953–1976*. Lanham, MD: University Press of America, 1995, pp. 13–14.

Chapter 4

1. With the advent of the Grand Ole Opry in 1925, a successful publishing industry already in place, and the establishment of brothers Owen and Harold Bradley's Film and Recording Studio in 1955 (later named

Quonset Hut Studio and Columbia Studio B)—the first major label recording studio on what became Music Row, Nashville, became known as "Music City USA." In 1957, RCA Studios began operation at the corner of 17th Avenue South and Hawkins Street, subsequently named RCA Studio B, reiterating the significance of the music industry, especially country music during the time.

2. In 1955, Kelly Miller Smith was president of Nashville's NAACP when the 1954 Supreme Court ruled against school segregation. In 1955, Smith and twelve other African American parents filed a federal lawsuit against segregation in the Nashville schools. As one of the city's most powerful and influential figures, Smith played an active role in the push for equity, including successful sit-ins at lunch counters in Nashville in the 1960s.
   For his leadership, *Time* magazine gave Smith the major credit for the city's transition away from Jim Crow. *Ebony* magazine also named him "One of America's Ten Most Outstanding Preachers" in 1954.
3. The female students in the freshman class of 1955 were pioneers, being the first class to gain formal admittance into the four-year medical program.
4. Howard University Medical School, established in 1868, was the first medical college founded to specifically educate African Americans.
5. Threonine is an essential amino acid that plays an important role in regulating protein balance in the body. Amino acids like threonine play a vital role in the structure of our bones, muscles, and skin. Because it is considered an "essential amino acid," which means the body does not synthesize the amino acid, we need to eat foods high in threonine to obtain it (American Chemical Society).
6. Interview with Dr. Audrey Forbes Manley, November 13, 2015.
7. Ibid.
8. Ibid.
9. Manley 2020 interview.
10. Ibid.

Chapter 5

1. Manley 2015 interview.
2. St. Mary's Mercy Hospital expanded over the early decades due to population growth in the city. When industries turned downward, people fled and the hospital became debt-ridden, enduring a slow but a steady decline until it finally closed in 1995.
3. St. Mary's Mercy Hospital was the birthplace for entertainers Michael, Janet, and the rest of the Jackson siblings.
4. Manley 2015 interview.
5. Ibid.
6. The condition occurs when you inherit the Hb C gene from one parent and the Hb S gene from the other. Individuals with Hb SC have symptoms similar to those of individuals with Hb SS.
7. Charles R. Drew University of Medicine and Science would also offer residencies after its inception in 1966, emphasizing service to the south central region of Los Angeles following the Watts riots.
8. The list of private historically Black graduate institutions was joined in 1966 by Charles R. Drew University of Medicine and Science in Willowbrook, California.
9. Manley 2015 interview.

Chapter 6

1. Ibid.
2. Ibid.
3. Ibid.
4. Ibid.
5. Ibid.
6. Ibid.
7. Manley 2020 interview.
8. Fontanelle is a "soft spot" of a newborn's skull. It is a unique feature that is important for the normal growth and development of a baby's brain and skull. Health teams, accordingly, routinely check baby's fontanelles during routine visits.
9. Manley 2015 interview.
10. Manley phone interview on Sunday, February 12, 2022.
11. Manley 2015 interview.
12. Ibid.

13. Ibid.
14. Manley 2020 interview.
15. In addition to being a breakthrough applicant as an African American, there were also disparaging practices in NIH grant-giving pertaining to female grant applicants and toward certain research topics. Dr. Manley's successful application was noteworthy on all three accounts.
16. Manley 2015 interview.
17. Ibid.
18. Ibid.
19. Ibid.

Chapter 7

1. Ibid.
2. Ibid.
3. Since passing the Social Security Act in 1935, the federal government through Title V, pledged support through State projects to improve the health, safety, and well-being of mothers and children. It was officially known as the Maternal and Child Health (MCH) Services Block Grant (Title V of the Social Security Act).
4. By the early 1960s the Blackstone Rangers, formed by Eugene Hairston and Jeff Fort (who became the leader) was made up of twelve to fifteen-year-olds from Blackstone Avenue in the Woodlawn area of Chicago's South Side. The group was organized to protect its members from intimidation by other area gangs. The traditional enemy was the Devil's Disciples, founded by thirteen-year-old David Barksdale in 1960 initially as the Black Disciple Nation. Both had grown greatly due to mergers with other gangs by the time Dr. Forbes assumed the helm of the clinic, and the rivalry had intensified to fatal proportions.
5. The King-assassination riots were also called the Holy Week Uprising when Washington, DC, Chicago, Baltimore, and Kansas City experienced some of the worst riots.
6. Mayor Richard J. Daley statement to reporters as repeated by James Coates, *Chicago Tribune*, December 19, 2007.
7. Manley interview.
8. Manley interview.
9. Dr. Forbes (Manley) considered the possibility that some of the men may have been engaged in mandatory military duty but felt, even if this was the case, there would have been a relative male presence at least in medical leadership in the Russian cities. This, she did not see.
10. Manley 2020 interview.
11. Dorothy Shepard Manley Hall at Spelman College was built in 1964 in honor of Dorothy Shepard Manley, the late wife of Dr. Albert Manley, fifth president of the College. Known as Manley Hall, the building was dedicated in Mrs. Manley's name for her assistance in planning the furnishing and décor for the first-year residence hall.
12. Mount Zion Hospital was originally established in San Francisco in 1887 as a community hospital. In 1976, the hospital opened the first alternative birth center in San Francisco, and ten years later opened the city's first hospital-based comprehensive women's health center.
13. During the mid-1960s, Haight-Ashbury was a magnet for young people seeking a free and self-determined life. The hippie movement's key thinkers and leaders lived here, including poet Allen Ginsberg; musicians Jerry Garcia, Jimi Hendrix, and Janis Joplin; and psychologist Timothy Leary. They pursued an alternative life there free of convention, consumption, and societal obligations. The streets overflowed with free music, drugs, and sex tolerated for the most part. Popular bands such as Jefferson Airplane, the Grateful Dead, and the Byrds gave free concerts. Thousands of young Americans and Europeans made pilgrimages to Haight-Ashbury during the 1960s.
14. Dr. Audrey Manley's efforts to improve preparatory opportunities for Spelman students in healthcare fields were continuations of her initial discussions on the subject with Dr. Albert Manley dating back to his arrival as president of Spelman when she was a student.
15. Manley 2015 interview.
16. The Albert E. Manley College Center replaced Morgan Hall, dedicated in 1973.
17. See "Testimonial Banquet at Morgan Hall, Spelman College, July 11, 1933" in the Neighborhood Union Collection, Atlanta University Center Robert W. Woodruff Library Archives Research Center. Note: Lugenia Hope, wife of Morehouse President John Hope, was honored for twenty-five years of social service through the Neighborhood Union, the organization she founded in 1908 that was chartered in 1911. It was women-led, and one of Atlanta's most important organizations for social services.

Chapter 8

1. Manley 2015 interview.
2. Audrey Manley indicated, for example, that properly disseminated information about the effective use of protection items and contraceptive options were deterrents to disease transmittal and unplanned pregnancies.
3. Manley 2020 interview.
4. *Spelman College Bulletin*, 1973, p. 14.
5. *Spelman Spotlight*, November 1974 (Vol. XLII, No. 3), p. 2.
6. Rev. Rates were consistently attributed with influencing the consistent moral and ethical foundation at the College in official Spelman writings such as the *Messenger*, website, and other sources.
7. A Spelman College statement on the legacy of Rev. Rates (recently deceased) appeared in a memorial post on the College webpage in 2015.
8. Rev. Rates made the comment publicly in 1991. When Audrey returned to her alma mater to receive an honorary doctor of laws degree.
9. Brenda D. Dalton served the Student Health Services at Spelman for decades.
10. The Josiah Macy Jr. Foundation boasts about being "the only national foundation dedicated solely to improving the education of health professionals."
11. The shadowing component of the Center became a critical part of student preparation for healthcare study. It became its own entity, currently being the Women in Science and Health (WISH) Shadowing Program.
12. Manley 2020 interview.

Chapter 9

1. James Edward Cheek (1932–2010) became the youngest president of Howard University at age thirty-six, and served for twenty years (1969–1989), during which time he befriended Albert Manley while he was president at Spelman.
2. Manley interview.
3. Manley interview.
4. Manley Feb. 12, 2022 interview.
5. Manley 2020 interview.
6. Manley 2020 interview.
7. Manley Feb 9, 2022 interview.
8. Manley Feb 9, 2022 interview.
9. Manley 2020 interview.
10. Manley 2015 interview.
11. By act of Congress, the USPHS Commissioned Corps is authorized as one of eight Uniformed Services of the US along with the US Army, US Air Force, US Marine Corps, US Navy, US Space Force, US Coast Guard, and the National Oceanic and Atmospheric Administration Commissioned Officer Corps (NOAA Commissioned Corps).
12. The BCOAG was chartered officially on February 7, 1990.

Chapter 10

1. Flag rank indicated the rank of a flag office—any of the officers in the navy or coast guard above captain.
2. The Cosmos Club is a private social club for women and men distinguished in science, literature, the arts, a learned profession, or public service. Individuals are elected to membership based on scholarship, creative genius, and intellectual distinction. The club boasts that three presidents, two vice presidents, a dozen Supreme Court justices, thirty-six Nobel Prize winners, sixty-one Pulitzer Prize winners, and fifty-five recipients of the Presidential Medal of Freedom have been members.
3. Dr. Koop was nominated by President Ronald Reagan in March 1981 and confirmed in November. He served two terms under Reagan. When President Bush was elected, Dr. Koop advised him he would resign effective October 1, 1989. He entered terminal leave status in July, and Dr. James Mason became Acting Surgeon General until March 9, 1990, when Dr. Antonia Coello Novello was appointed.
4. Regarding the longer term cost of AIDS assistance, Dr. Manley pointed out: "We're still paying for it. We did not ask for sixteen billion dollars overnight and say, 'Here, put some money in it.' We were estimating what it was going to cost. It has cost more. More than twenty years have passed and we are still paying for AIDS. We are still buying medication. At least we got the vaccine. So, it was projecting where the AIDS epidemic was going to go. You had to look at it in the long run."

5. The 2008 Nobel Prize in Medicine was awarded to Montagnier and Françoise Barré-Sinoussi for the discovery of HIV. They shared the Prize with Harald zur Hausen, who discovered that human papilloma viruses can cause cervical cancer.
6. Dr. Manley thought David Satcher was quite brilliant but that his experiences for the most being from predominantly White institutions after his undergraduate experience at Morehouse did not attune him to the unique nuances of minority institutions. She felt this was also because he came through on the cusp of integration.
7. Vanderbilt already wanted to leave Nashville General because they were looking to build in the suburbs where population growth was occurring. They also were intent on operating satellite clinics across the city. Their future goals made the arrangement proposed by Dr. Satcher a smoother and more mutually feasible solution.
8. The NHSC is a federal program administered by the HRSA that "provide scholarships and loan repayment to healthcare professionals practicing at approved sites located in/or serving Health Professional Shortage Areas (HPSAs) throughout the US."
9. Hurricane Katrina became the costliest natural disaster in 2005 at $81 billion, surpassing Hurricane Andrew.
10. In Florida, the death toll was in the twenties, more than 250,000 people were left homeless, 82,000 businesses were destroyed or badly damaged, 100,000 residents of south Dade County left permanently, and the largest wetland in the US, the Florida Everglades, suffered severe damage resulting in environmental implications of major proportions.
11. The CCRF was established by the Office of the Surgeon General (OSG) in 1994. Operational management for the CCRF was transferred to the Office of Emergency Preparedness (OEP) in October 1997, at which time a CCRF Workgroup was established to develop a mission statement and operations plan. Following the 9/11 terrorist attacks and the anthrax attacks, OEP became the Office of Emergency Response (OER) and was transferred to the fledgling Department of Homeland Security. CCRF was concurrently transferred back to OSG in March 2003. CCRF was subsequently subsumed under the new Office of Force Readiness and Deployment (OFRD) in 2004. In 2013, OFRD was renamed the Readiness and Deployment Operations Group (Red Dog). In 2019, the name was changed to the Readiness and Deployment Branch (RDB), which is its current official name.

Chapter 11

1. Manley Feb.12, 2022 interview.
2. Manley July 8, 2020 interview.
3. Dr. Elder faced harsh criticism from conservatives in Congress for her insistence on bringing controversial and difficult topics up for debate. After fifteen months of political battles, she stepped down as US Surgeon General and returned to academia.
4. Peter Buxtun, a former venereal disease investigator with the PHS, shared information on the study's unethical practices to Associated Press reporter Jean Heller. The story broke on July 25, 1972, and sparked outcries nationwide, prompting Congressional hearings that led to federal legislation strengthening guidelines for protection of human subjects in research. The PHS defended the project, but it was closed immediately. There had been 600 participants—399 with the disease and 201 in the control group. After forty years, twenty-eight of the 399 men with syphilis had died of the disease, another 100 men had died of complications related to the disease, forty had passed the disease on to their wives, and nineteen children of diseased men had been born with congenital syphilis.
5. Since that date, more than twenty million dollars in grants and pledges have been made to Tuskegee University to help establish and operate the Center. Ten million of these dollars have been given to the Center, to be used over a five-year period by the Centers for Disease Control and Prevention (CDC).
6. Manley interview July 8, 2020.
7. The bioethics center was devoted to engaging the sciences, humanities, law, and religious faiths in the exploration of the core moral issues that underlie research and medical treatment of African Americans and other underserved people. The Center was launched two years after President Clinton's apology to the nation, the survivors of the Syphilis Study, Tuskegee University, and Tuskegee/Macon County for the US PHS medical experiment.
8. The NSF survey pointed out that Spelman College as a considerably smaller, all-female institution in the south, the achievement in science fields was impressive. The study indicated that Howard University, which placed number one, has a coeducational enrollment of more than three times that of Spelman with a graduate program, medical college, and hospital.
9. Manley 2015 interview.
10. Ibid.

11. Ibid.
12. Ibid.
13. The account surrounding the death of Dr. Albert Manley at their Jamaica home was initially stated during the 2015 interview and was repeated twice in the interview from 2020 using essentially the identical terms.

Chapter 12

1. From Eloise Abernathy Alexis, "Sister to Sister: The Undaunted Spirit," in *Spelman Messenger*, Summer/Fall 2002, p. 12.
2. Dr. Audrey Forbes Manley interview with author May 13, 2023.
3. Ibid.
4. Ibid.
5. Dr. Audrey Forbes Manley became the eighth president of Spelman College effective July 1, 1997; however, she was ceremonially installed in a traditional official service held in October 1998. These ceremonies are customarily planned during the first year of a president's term and occur during the fall of the following year. Her loyal former Special Assistant from PHS, Captain Steve Moore, was on hand "to help if and where he might be needed."
6. The Intergovernmental Personnel Act Mobility Program (IPA) provides for the temporary assignment of personnel between the federal government and state and local governments, colleges and universities, Indian tribal governments, federally funded research and development centers, and other eligible organizations.
7. Barbara Boone was interviewed by the author on November 27, 2022.
8. Boone interview.
9. Spelman College, *Reflections*, 1998, p. 3.
10. See Dr. Audrey Forbes Manley, "A Charge to Keep I Have," Inaugural Address in *Spelman Messenger*, Winter/Spring 1999, p. 5.
11. Spelman College, *Reflections*, 1999, p. 2.
12. Manley 2015 interview.
13. Manley phone conversation with author, August 2020.
14. Spelman was founded in 1881 as the Atlanta Baptist Female Seminary. Founders Harriet E. Giles and Sophia B. Packard, along with a group of Baptist women, organized the Women's American Baptist Home Mission Society as an auxiliary to the American Baptist Home Mission Society. In 1884, the name was changed to Spelman Seminary in honor of Mrs. Laura Spelman Rockefeller and her parents Harvey Buel and Lucy Henry Spelman, John D. Rockefeller having been the initial donor to the seminary. Spelman Seminary officially became Spelman College in 1924.
15. The New Packard Hall renovation and addition was recognized with the 2004 Atlanta Urban Design Commission Award of Excellence for Historic Preservation and the 2007 Georgia American Institute of Architects (AIA) Design with Brick—second Place Honor Award.
16. Iyamu, Joyce, *The Spelman Spotlight*, April 27, 2001, Vol. XLV, No. 7, p. 1.
17. Manley interview 2020.
18. The title of Rev. Rate's book was taken from a line in the Spelman Hymn. It is a prayer that the Chapel will never be destroyed by time or memory.
19. Manley interview with author.
20. The Continuing Education Student Association (CESA), established in 1989, voted in 2003 to change the association's name to The Pauline E. Drake Scholars (PEDS) as a tribute to Dr. Drake for her longtime support as advisor to the organization.
21. Manley 2015 interview.
22. Dr. Manley recounted the incident in the Manley 2022 interview, and reiterated in subsequent conversations how important expansion possibilities became as she settled into her presidential duties.
23. Dr. Manley served as Chair during the formation meetings. Once incorporated, CPI, Inc. showed Robert D. Flanigan as Principal Officer and the Main Address as 350 Spelman Lane, SW, Atlanta, GA 30314.
24. Dr. Audrey Forbes Manley interview February 9, 2022.
25. Manley interview 2020.
26. Dr. Gayles subsequently wrote two additional books, *In Praise of Teachers* (2003) and *Conversations with Gwendolyn Brooks* (2003), and oversaw publications from the SIS program.
27. Dr. Gayles began her teaching career at Spelman as an instructor during the academic year 1963–1964.
28. SIS published two Student-Edited Volumes of *Their Memories, Our Treasure: Conversations with African American Women of Wisdom* and *They Saw The Sun First*, An online journal of Age-Focused Research and Writing Across The Disciplines.
29. Spelman discontinued the Cosby Endowed Chair and informed the public in an announcement on

December 14, 2014, issuing the following statement: "The William and Camille Olivia Hanks Cosby Endowed Professorship was established to bring positive attention and accomplished visiting scholars to Spelman College in order to enhance our intellectual, cultural, and creative life; however, the current context prevents us from continuing to meet these objectives fully. Consequently, we will suspend the program until such time that the original goals can again be met."

30. According to college documents, following a rigorous application process that included the submission of a 157-page General Report and a three-day site visit, Spelman was granted a chapter of Phi Beta Kappa on September 27, 1997, at the Thirty-Eighth Triennial Meeting of the Phi Beta Kappa Council in Chicago.
31. Comments by Paul R. Jones to the author February 15, 2001.
32. Dr. Audrey Manley during her retirement announcement on October 11, 2001.
33. Over four years, 70 million dollars of the funds raised by Dr. Manley were private and federal funds.
34. Dr. Hopps was quoted in the article, "Spelman College President Announces Retirement" in the November 7, 2001 edition of *Diverse: Issues in Higher Education*.
35. Statement on the mission of The Trumpet Awards by Xernona Clayton Brady who initiated the ceremony established in 1992 with the full support of Turner Broadcasting System (TBS) founder and then-CEO, Ted Turner. A decade later, she became the Founder, President, and CEO of the Trumpet Awards Foundation, Inc. and Creator and Executive Producer of the Foundation's Trumpet Awards until the event was acquired in December 2016 by Bounce TV. Bounce TV now owns, produces, and world premieres the annual Trumpet Awards.
36. Statement during the presentation of the Trumpet Award to Dr. Audrey Manley.
37. TBS statement when Dr. Manley was presented the award.
38. The inscription on the plaque reads: "Donated Through the Generous Contributions of Spelman College Alumnae and Friends." This indicates contributions were made by friends of Dr. Manley, friends of the College, or both.
39. Eloise Alexis in *Spelman Messenger*, Summer/Fall 2002.

Epilogue

1. The interview was conducted November 9, 2020.
2. The EDGE Program went national in 2004 and since that time has grown into a national program whose participants have received well over 100 PhDs in the mathematical sciences. Former Spelman mathematics department professor and Chair Sylvia Bozeman and Helen Herrmann, professor emeritus at Bryn Mawr Rhonda Hughes, administer the EDGE Foundation.
3. Written for President Audrey Forbes Manley in honor of her Inauguration on October 25, 1998. ©Amena J. Brown 1998.

www.ingramcontent.com/pod-product-compliance
Lightning Source LLC
Chambersburg PA
CBHW031550260326
41914CB00002B/354
* 9 7 8 1 9 6 6 2 1 4 4 5 8 *